MOVE TOWARD
LOVE

Visionary Insight
PRESS

See, beautiful
Stay the you are.
Soul that you shine
and Always Stars!
like the Stars!
Deb
2014

MOVE TOWARD
LOVE

Move Toward LOVE

Visionary Insight Press, LLC, P.O. Box 30484, Spokane, WA 99223

Visionary Insight Press, the Visionary Insight Press logo and its individual parts are trademarks of Visionary Insight Press, LLC

Compiled by: Nancy A Newman and Lisa Hardwick-Peplow
Editor: Lisa Hardwick-Peplow
Project Director: Lisa Hardwick-Peplow
Back cover photo credit: Captured Moments Photography, Karen Seargeant, Gina Myers Photography, Allan Forest, Curious Coyote Creative, Expressions by Ashton Photography, JC Penney Portrait Studio, Heidi Phillips, Transition Studios, Deb Hagen Photography and Digital Art, David Vernon, Jose Corella Photography, Karen Leonard, Jenny Paul, Addison A. Cumberbatch–Willie Alleyne Associates.

Profound joy is
like a magnet
that indicates
the path of life.

~ MOTHER TERESA

Table of Contents

Foreword

by Dr. Patricia Crane

We all know it when we feel it—but how to define love when there are so many expressions of it in different forms? The dictionary definitions seem woefully inadequate: *an intense feeling of deep affection or attraction based on sexual desire.* Spiritual teachers, philosophers and poets have certainly tried, and their words give us a glimpse of the true depth of agape (unconditional love) and eros (romantic love.) Rather than define love, the authors in this book take you on their journeys to experience it. Their ultimate focus is on unconditional love—for themselves, others, and the situations in their lives. They found joy in being with themselves and learning to love who they are.

When we look at a small baby and watch him or her smile and giggle, burp and frown, we can see the promise of a wonderful life. Our hearts seem to naturally open when we see a new baby. The innocence of that child shines forth and we want it to experience only the joys of life. Perhaps our hearts open so easily for a baby because we can feel the openness and unconditional love shining forth from that child. A baby has not yet put limits on its ability and willingness to love.

Sadly, as we grow we learn that love is usually conditional. We discover we are loved if we act as expected by the adults around us and so we strive to please others. We learn about fears and judgments and slowly our hearts begin to close. Our later life task, if we are open to it, becomes stripping away the layers that have covered up the heart and closed it off to unconditional love.

The unconscious mind absorbs everything, tucks it away and sets it up for future experiences. We begin to create stories in our heads about our worthiness to receive love, what being "in love" means and what relationships are like. Then our life experiences reflect these stories. During training workshops I teach in Louise Hay's philosophy, I use a pair of oversized sunglasses to demonstrate how we all have filters (oh so many of them!) in the unconscious mind that block our ability to love unconditionally, and also our ability to live an empowered life in all areas. Especially in the area of relationships, the participants can easily understand (and sometimes even laugh about!) how many of the differences with their partners occur because of these filters! Understanding our own filters allows us to find greater compassion and love for others and ourselves.

Thousands of years ago Jesus said, "Love your neighbor as yourself." Until recently, the "as yourself" part seems to have been forgotten by many people. Loving yourself was seen as selfish and narcissistic rather than empowering. When you truly love yourself, you let go of the need to please others all the time, to be perfect, and to try and fit into a mold created by others. You create new and empowering inner messages for yourself. You take risks to find the authentic life for you. You learn to love yourself in your full range: the positive parts of your personality, as well as the rough edges. Even comedienne Lucille Ball came to that conclusion, "Love yourself first and everything else falls into line. You really have to love yourself to get anything done in this world."

Life has often been compared to a roller coaster. The highs of love, joy, and adventure are easy to accept. It is the dips of the roller coaster that challenge us to choose our reaction. We may be jolted by an unexpected illness or death, a partner asking for a divorce, or a betrayal. How to respond? One can choose to respond with anger, depression, and resignation, or with acceptance, and yes, love.

How do we move toward love? We can't usually jump directly from fear and judgment and anger to love. That is why the title of this book, *Move Toward Love,* is so apt. We take steps, we have insights, we are guided by wise others and situations. A favorite spiritual course of mine, *A Course in Miracles*, reminds us that we don't need to know how, we just need the willingness to love. It also tells us that forgiveness is the key to happiness and love. When you have that willingness, Spirit begins to guide you to the insights and experiences you need.

The authors in this book share honestly and openly with you about their journeys as they confront situations that challenged them to open their hearts to more love. Moving toward love for them involved many lessons and insights. Take the time to make the journey with them as they describe their struggles and breakthroughs. There are wise words you will want to highlight as insights for your own life path. They will encourage you by example to reflect on questions for your life: Who do I need to forgive? How do I make empowered choices for my life? How can I love myself and others more fully? They remind you to find the gift in every situation, and that you always have the power to choose.

May you have joy and miracles on your own journey to greater love for yourself, others and the adventure of Life.

Patricia J. Crane, Ph.D
Author of *Ordering from the Cosmic Kitchen*
www.drpatriciacrane.com
www.healyourlifetraining.com

Mavis Hogan

MAVIS HOGAN is a business owner and event coordinator, living in Spokane Washington. Mavis is a lifelong student of the Metaphysical and loves people and meeting new people. She enjoys planning events and gatherings for like- minded people in the metaphysical community. Her business website is www.themagicmysticaltour.com and every month you will find something new going on there. If it is metaphysical it can become a class or workshop! If you have an interest in it she will try to bring it to life! She has a husband, three children, six grandchildren and an apricot poodle. She enjoys reading and writing and spending time with her family and friends. Her Motto: The Older I Get the Better I Like Me and My Life!

mavishogan@comcast.net
www.themagicmysticaltour.com

Move-Toward-Love

MOVE: to pass from one place to another

TOWARD: in the direction of

LOVE: an intense personal attachment or affection

~ RANDOM HOUSE WEBSTER'S DICTIONARY

(©1993)

As I read the meaning of these three words I thought, "Oh my, what a powerful thought in just one short sentence."

To pass from one place to another in the direction of an intense, personal attachment or affection.

PERFECT.

To me, this said I could pass from a place of non-love from others, including Myself, in the direction of an intense personal attachment or affection of love IF ONLY from myself, and in finding it FOR myself, I may find it from others, or for others.

When I became a single parent in 1977 after the birth of my second child, I was a scared little girl. I say little girl because I was only 23 years old. I know I thought I was so grown up when I married at 18 and started my family, but I had no idea what was in store for me. I thought love would hold it all together. What I didn't know was that one person, loving for two, was not nearly enough, and that *that* one person was loving the wrong person. Instead of loving myself first, I poured all my heart and soul into the man (boy) that was my husband, who at the same time had no idea how to love anyone either. So, yes, looking back at what 23 is, it is not as grown up as I thought it was. When I see someone 23 now I think, oh you're so young. Live your life. Go out and see the world and find out who you are. Learn to love yourself so that you can love others, so that they too may love you.

Now my own children are grown and gone and they have been replaced with grandchildren. I see these children and grandchildren of mine going through their adult struggles or teenage struggles, but can I say any of them are really loving themselves? I see young adults working to make a family and building careers. I see teenagers struggling with body images and the younger ones not far behind with issues of their own.

Nobody actually taught us to love ourselves. There is a bit more help out there today for that than there used to be, but where do you find it?

The other day I was watching a medical show where they were talking about the differences in men and women's brains. (I will do my best to describe it to you in my own words.) The outside covering of the brain is called the Grey Matter, this is where we all think, where the thoughts come in. Where the difference comes in is in the White Matter found in the center of the brain. Women have a huge amount of White Matter compared to men. The White Matter is where our thoughts go after leaving the Grey Matter. For women that means we start thinking (sometimes too hard), about the stuff that entered our Grey Matter. So in thinking about it so hard we end up worrying, crying, carrying stuff we don't need too, etc. Men on the other hand don't. They spend more time just thinking about the stuff in their Grey Matter and analyzing it. Not worrying about it or stressing out.

So take a young boy who has gone through puberty and is thinking about girls and sex all the time. That is all he thinks about. Sex. He may know he likes girls and that is all he needs to know. Now take a girl, who has reached the age that she thinks about boys and sex. She now thinks about sex as love, commitment, being together forever, marriage, babies, happily ever after. She may wear makeup, dye her hair, and choose her clothes based on what she thinks a boy is thinking about and wants to see. She may acquire a bad body image and lose weight or end up with any number of self -esteem issues, mainly because she spent too much time in her White Matter.

Today I see young girls as early as thirteen and fourteen, yearning for love or attention from boys. Girls who think they are so grown up, and feel so grown up, looking for attention from a boy who has absolutely no idea about themselves or their feelings, let alone about girls and *their* feelings.

What has happened to us that we think we need love and approval from others in order to be complete anyway?

 It is never too late to be who you might have been!

~ GEORGE ELIOT

Now 35 years later I can see how true these words are. You know you wanted to FEEL something, BE something, or DO something.

You may have wanted to be noticed, or give of yourself in some way.

You simply wanted to make your mark in the world.

In my case I know that I spent more time wishing for others to be different or do different or treat me different, when really all along it was ME who needed to be different. There just were no tools that I knew of for learning how to do that. Why did we settle for what we got? Why didn't we demand more of ourselves? Why didn't families teach it to their children?

If there is one thing I can tell young people, it is to NOT to look for others to make you who you want to be. You have to do it for yourself. No one in your life can make you who you are meant to be. LEARN TO LOVE YOURSELF!

 If at first you don't succeed, you are probably lucky!

~ MARGARET L CLEMENT

Yes lucky! If the first thing you set out to do didn't work, it caused you to try something else. Only the next time hopefully you were a bit more wary and dug deeper or tried harder. You did not want to come to that place again where something didn't go right. So if something felt right the next time, you made sure it WAS right.

Imagine all the possibilities there are in one single life! Try as many as you can! LIVE! TRY! FAIL! Yes, fail. If you stopped trying after your first attempt, imagine all the things you would miss. Life isn't a destination, it's a journey. And one thing I have learned through my experiences or in talking to others about theirs is, there is no THERE! You do NOT arrive some place one day and say, "Oh, Finally I am here!" No, everyday there are new choices and decisions to make to aid in the trek of your particular journey through this life. A journey to be lived to the fullest potential you can. Don't stop! Don't EVER stop! There is so much out there to love and so many ways TO Love. And in your pursuit you will meet others along the way and share what you know and they will share with you. Be your own best friend. Share yourself with you.

 I am still learning how to take joy in all the people I am, how to use all my selves in the service of what I believe, how to accept when I fail and rejoice when I succeed.

~ AUDRE LORDE

Yes I can accept when I fail. It may hurt or make me sad for a time, but every day is a new day to start over or try again. There are many faces to the person that we are. We get to try and fail and try again. Why not. And, if I succeed, yes I can celebrate that and know that I am on the right path. But also know that there is not only One Path. Your options are endless! Go for the Gold! Love and Celebrate You and Your Life!!

The Options Are Endless

 You may have a fresh start any moment you choose, for this thing that we call "failure" is not the falling down, but the staying down.

~ MARY PICKFORD

There is no failure in trying. Just don't stay down. Get up and Get Moving. Don't waste your time on what ifs. If a friendship dies, a marriage ends, do not for one moment think you are the only one. There are so many people out there today, who took a chance on themselves again and again. They didn't love themselves EVERY single day! No. But they got up and brushed themselves off. They dared to try again.

I remember when my son was just out of high school, and trying to figure himself out, I suggested to him that he might try taking some night classes at the local community college. Like a six week course in cooking, or a three week course in auto mechanics, or a four week course in guitar. The options are endless. Try it all. See what feels good. How do you know you don't want to play a guitar if you have never held one or strummed one or heard a tune coming from it that YOU have made. The very joy of something may just be in something you had no idea about until you try. Only YOU know what feels good. Try it, if it doesn't feel good, start over or try something else.

 I don't want to get to the end of my life and find that I just lived the length of it. I want to have lived the width of it as well.

~ DIANE ACKERMAN

At 23 years of age I had no idea what was out there to do. I didn't know where to start. Now today, I would say GOOGLE IT! If you want to know about something, look it up, read about it. Discover everything you can about it. Volunteer. Try it. You can always quit, or start over, or try something else. Just try. Get up, get moving, and get thinking about SOMETHING. While you are trying, reading, learning, and searching, you find love. Yes love, a love, FOR something. Loving something leads you to a place of others loving the same things that you do. You share your joy with them, *that* is loving. You are sharing the love of the thing you have in common and you are sharing the love of a person. Friendships grow from that shared experience.

The purpose of life, after all, is to live it, to taste experience to the utmost, to reach out eagerly and without fear for newer and richer experience.

~ ELEANOR ROOSEVELT

"AHHHHHHHHH" Bliss

 BLISS: a supreme happiness in something. Heaven. Paradise.

~ RANDOM HOUSE WEBSTER'S DICTIONARY

(© 1993)

Once you have found your BLISS, you can begin to contribute all of you to any relationship you may have. No matter if it is in work, in pleasure, or in people. Everyone needs to find BLISS. Bliss for something.

I was in my forties before I really knew that word. But once I discovered it I couldn't put it down. I loved the meaning of it, and I especially LOVED the sound of it. Oh, to find your Bliss as self-help authors suggested. Once you found it, how wonderful life would be. The first time I heard someone say "What is your Bliss?" I thought hmmmmmmmm, "What is it? Well I don't know." Then someone suggested, "You must find your Bliss, or Follow your Bliss." Well silly me, because I had such low self- esteem about myself I thought, "Well I can't do that! How Dare I take the time to focus on me, after all there is my husband and kids, and my job. How could I possibly take time from all of that to concentrate on what I may want?"

I thought about that word a lot over the next few weeks and realized, if not me, then who was going to figure out MY Bliss!? (and I truly did love and adore the sound of that word! And I am no longer embarrassed to admit that.) What if I was missing out on something that it appeared OTHERS were giving themselves, and I was too busy with LIFE, to find it for ME!?

For me I have discovered that the search IS my bliss. For me, my happiness is in learning new things, trying new things or new experiences or meeting new people or going new places. Every day is bliss-full. There are new choices to be made or new things to experience each and every day! And most of all, my family didn't suffer from me taking that search. From what I figure, they were better for it as well. Once I started learning things or trying things or doing things for me, I became better for it. They were only on the receiving end of the new improved ME!

 Every small, positive change we can make in ourselves repays us in confidence in the future.

~ALICE WALKER

Beginning with the plug in cover I replaced as my first independent act after my divorce, as silly as it sounds, led me to believing in myself. It began to slowly start the process to building my confidence toward the future me that would one day recover and be a healthy functioning adult. I started to love myself that day as a silly little outlet cover was replaced by MY HANDS and I wished for a just a moment there had been someone there to applaud me, or pat me on the back for my efforts and to look at me and say, "Look at you, you did it all by yourself." But actually I believe it made ME love me more that I had to applaud myself. So at first when I changed that silly little outlet cover, I cried. After all, wasn't I led to believe by my ex-husband that I couldn't make it on my own? And wasn't this the proof I needed that yes I could!? For some, they may have needed more proof, but for me, it may have been merely a plug in cover but it may as well have been an entire house. Here it is

35 years later and I can feel it like it was yesterday. So yes, I cried for the scared me, who was now setting out on the process of making it on my own. When I finished crying, I smiled. Smiled because I knew I was going to be okay. I was beginning to Love myself and trust me with myself. "We" were going to be just fine.

So whatever curve ball life or the people in it want to throw at you, just imagine: As you Move Toward Love, and as you search out Your Bliss, you may just happen to find someone doing that very thing as well. They too will be trying to build or rebuild a life. They may be just beginning or starting over but, you will meet and share experiences. You could turn each other on to new choices that you never even thought of before. You could grow together. You could learn together. You could Move Toward Love, together.

As I Move Toward Love throughout my life I find just a little bit more of myself. Each person, place, or thing that moved me to love it or them, showed me who I am, what I can do and what I am capable of. Thank you to this life that has treated me well, with all its ups and downs, I have come to be the best ME I can be. I can only look forward to whatever comes next with Hope and Gratitude for anything and everything that lets me continue this journey of self - love and love for others.

I dedicate this book to my mother Wilma who died April 4th, 2013 and my brother in law Loren who died seven days later on April 11th, 2013. I hope they know I loved them. Also to the people I have loved and who have loved me I want to say that the world is better for having you in it. Without any of you I would not be who I am today.

~ Mavis Hogan

As far as we can discern,
the sole purpose of
human existence is to
kindle a light in the
darkness of mere being.

~ CARL JUNG

Lisa Hardwick-Peplow

LISA HARDWICK-PEPLOW is a Best-Selling Author, Speaker, Workshop Trainer, Publishing Consultant and an advocate for Self Discovery. She is passionate about sharing tools to empower others to live their best lives.

She lives in the same small university town where she was born, Charleston, Illinois, to be near her three adult sons and their families. After years of extensive travel, Lisa learned that her treasure always resided where her journey began.

lisa@lisahardwick.com
www.lisahardwick.com

Vibration Elevation

The first time I was introduced to a Vibrational Scale model, it was as if someone suddenly flipped on a light switch! I was so excited about what I had learned that I immediately created a specialized workshop titled Vibration Elevation™ so I could acquaint others to this incredible information. The basic principle of the Vibrational Scale is pretty simple; *Our soul is love and when we move toward love, up the Vibrational Scale, we are actually moving away from fear. All negative emotions are fear-based so the concept is to raise our vibration up the Vibrational Scale toward love, our soul.*

My intention is to share with you the principles of Vibrations and provide *how-to* information, as taught by many spiritual teachers such as the incredible David Hawkins, so you may choose to elevate *your* Vibrations. When we learn to do this and we immediately began to move toward love and away from fear, the benefits include experiencing a higher level of well-being, joy, creativity, wisdom, and authenticity. We become who we were created to be before we were exposed to the fear we learned. The fear of not being smart enough, good enough, pretty enough, handsome enough, etc. Are you ready to feel more joy? More love? I bet you are! I was too! Allow me to explain just a bit more and then we'll get started! Okay?

What *are* Vibrations? Vibrations can be thought of as "your mood" or how you are *feeling*. So, when you hear someone say "I'm in a bad mood" ... what they are really saying is "I want to elevate my Vibrations." And even then there's still a little more to it, which you'll learn in this chapter.

I think you'll find this quite interesting; Did you know physicists believe the building blocks of the universe are tiny, vibrating loops of subatomic particles named *strings*? And since *everything* in our universe is ultimately composed of these vibrating strings, *it follows that everything* has energy and *everything* vibrates. The difference is, some things vibrate at a low frequency, like a desk, and other things vibrate at a much higher frequency, like a human being.

When people vibrate at a low frequency, they *don't* feel good. And when people vibrate at a high frequency, they *do* feel good. And then, there are some who vibrate at a really high frequency, and they feel GREAT! (Those are the people I LOVE to hang out with!) So in essence, you now understand that vibrating at a low level equates to "feeling bad" and vibrating at a high level results in "feeling good." You're getting so good at this!

Let's think about this scenario for a moment:

Think of those people you know who *always* have problems in their lives. It seems every time they turn around something "bad" happens *to* them. Perhaps you've noticed they are oftentimes sick with colds, sinus issues, aches and pains, or they may even have a dis-ease. Or another scenario may be something such as one year they were going through a divorce, the next year they lost their job, etc. But whatever the circumstances, they are always in some sort of crisis. Do you know anyone like this?

You may also notice these people often choose behaviors such as being a workaholic, or a food addict, or relationship dependent, or abusing alcohol and/or drugs, or needing constant attention as a means of relief from the recurrent catastrophes in their lives. But we all know those types of coping methods for feeling better are not healthy or ever sustainable for a long period of time, right? People such as this are vibrating at a low frequency and don't feel well. In fact, many feel so bad that it's painful to them both emotionally and physically. Don't you think if they knew superior coping strategies they would choose those tactics rather than engage in self-destructive behavior? It's clear in most cases low vibrational people are living a fear-based life instead of moving toward love. Wouldn't you agree?

Now, let's further think about how *you* feel when you are around those who are vibrating at a low frequency. Do you feel drained of energy? This can be challenging when you have some type of special relationship with them such as a relative, a partner, your teacher or even your boss. When we surround ourselves without healthy boundaries and protection with those who vibrate at a low frequency we can take on their energy, and in turn, attract more of what they are. In short, we become more like them. We all know we attract what we are like. Like attracts like. Perhaps you may be thinking at this time, "Oh my goodness, *I* am vibrating at a low frequency level!" Perhaps you are ... but don't worry ... I've got you covered! Remember, we are all doing the best we can do with the knowledge and tools we have and when you read further you will learn some new tools. Here, allow me to assist you with your tool belt ... we're going to be filling it up very soon!

Now, let's consider another scenario:

Think of those you know who are always smiling and upbeat, and it seems *everything* always works out for them (*because it usually does!*) Do you think those you know who are high vibrational didn't have the same level of life challenges as those who are vibrating at a lower level? Actually, I've met some of the most incredible, high vibrational people who have experienced some of the most difficult life challenges you could ever imagine. My journey led me to those who have experienced cancer, HIV, or buried a child. I've been introduced to others who have learned they were betrayed after many years of marriage, those who have been through the loss of their mate through an act of suicide, those who have experienced financial ruin who literally went from riches to rags. But despite all the obstacles placed in their path, they were people who had the tools to vibrate at a high frequency level and chose to utilize those strategies to have a higher level of well-being, joy, creativity, wisdom, and live an authentic life while making a conscious choice to move toward love and away from fear.

Here is an insightful nugget to help you understand Vibrations even *more* deeply. Our bodies have tens of trillions of cells and every single cell must vibrate. The higher the frequency of vibration we choose to feel, then the higher the level of cellular vibration and healthier cells we have, and the better we feel both emotionally and physically. Conversely, the lower the frequency of vibration we have, the less healthy our cells are, and the worse we feel. It is apparent that when we feel bad, our cells are infected by such things that show up in our lives like dis-ease, obesity, depression, anger, etc. In other words, all things we associate with being *negative*. And you know what else? Oftentimes, people who are low vibrational are agitated by those who are high vibrational. Put another way, when we have negativity in our lives, our cells are vibrating at a low frequency causing us to feel depleted and exhausted, and the result is ... we feel terrible. And, when our lives are filled with love, joy, peace, and gratitude, and our mind, body, and spirit are in a healthy balance due to utilizing tools we've learned to cause our cells to vibrate at a high frequency ... we feel good! I have a feeling you're really getting it now! Am I right?

Ok then! Now I am going to share with you a tidbit about recent a breakthrough that has allowed researchers to measure a person's frequency on a specific Vibrational Scale. The scale works in a way as if you would imagine you have a scale of 1 to 1,000, with 1,000 being the highest state a human is able to reach. If you reach this level you would be a Master in Enlightenment. At the lowest end of the scale is someone who is obviously struggling in all aspects of their being. To determine where people are on the scale, researchers use muscle testing and kinesiology. As you can see, heavy emotions like shame and guilt vibrate at low frequencies, while feelings like joy, peace, and enlightenment vibrate at high, uplifting frequencies. The measurements on this particular scale are as follows:

700 +	Enlightenment	175	Pride
600	Peace	150	Anger
540	Joy	125	Desire
500	Love	100	Fear
400	Reason	75	Grief
350	Acceptance	50	Apathy
310	Willingness	30	Guilt
250	Neutrality	20	Shame
200	Courage		

One of the most important steps to elevating our Vibrations is *awareness*. We must be aware of our frequency level and how that level is affecting our lives before we are able to raise ourselves to a higher frequency. It's oftentimes a good decision to figure out where we are before we know where we need to go. Just take a moment and choose to be aware of your frequency on the Vibrational Scale.

Well it's time! Now I am going to share 20 tools to elevate your vibrations! These strategies are being shared in no particular order *and* once we are finished you may think of some things that would work for you that aren't even *on* the list, and that's great! Write them down and incorporate them into your own life!

1. MOVEMENT: Exercise isn't solely for your body—it benefits your mind. Physical activity will raise your vibration and promote healthy brainwave patterns and great circulation throughout your entire nervous system. When you choose to start moving, whether it be a simple walk or turning on music and dancing, you will immediately begin raising your vibrations. When I feel low, I visualize stagnate energy in my body, and I know movement will help get it moving to bring it up and then out! And surely enough—every time I choose to move, I feel so much better.

2. INTENTION: Simply setting an intention to elevate your vibrations will indeed elevate your vibrations! When we choose positive intentions, we program ourselves to have a positive mind. When we develop habits such as good intentions we raise our vibration frequency. Not only that, but we will naturally attract like-minded people, which will result in a higher quality of well-being due to the fact that much of our vibration level has to do with the relationships we have attracted.

3. MEDITATION: There are many forms of meditation that are beneficial for elevating your vibrations. Find a style that personally works well for you and enjoy the many paths to well-being meditation has to offer!

4. NATURE: Get outside! Whether that means a walk around your neighborhood or a drive in the country, being near nature oftentimes allows us to experience a deep peace and oneness with life. Maybe now you better understand what those "Tree Hugging People" are all about?

5. TRUTH: Always tell the truth to live a high vibrational life. Each and every time you tell the truth, you elevate your vibrations. High vibrational people don't lie due to the fact their intentions are to be true to themselves, to others, and to humanity as a whole.

6. HEALTHY FRIENDS: Find and spend time with friends who are in alignment with your beliefs and values. When we have friends like this, they will keep us accountable for the choices to live our best lives.

Cherish these friends and make it a habit to share memorable times with them on a consistent basis.

7. INNER CHILD: Focus on what you loved doing as a child around the age of ten. Was it reading? Creating art? Singing? Playing make-believe? Having fun with a particular game? Do it! When you purposefully have fun with your inner-child you elevate your vibrations.

8. FORGIVE YOURSELF: Forgiving yourself can be extremely challenging at times, especially if you are operating from a low vibrational frequency. This is a time to be aware that *every* human being has had incidents in their lives they needed to forgive themselves for and to remember that at the time, they were doing the best they could with what they knew. Understand that in order to elevate your vibrations and move up higher on the scale, you must be more nurturing with yourself. Make a conscious decision to release any negative emotions that no longer serve you. Forgive yourself.

9. RESPECT YOURSELF: Is the Aretha Franklin song R*E*S*P*E*C*T* running through your mind right now? Good! It is vital to have respect for ourselves and our actions, and when we do, it raises our level of LOVE for ourselves. And when we have love for ourselves, we will then be able to love others authentically. And an even higher level is to learn to be "in love" with ourselves, *then* you'll be able to be "in love" with another more authentically!

10. GRATITUDE: Take a moment and simply focus on all you are grateful for. Think of the people, items you need and want, and even the smallest of niceties like a wonderful cup of coffee and elevate from there! You may want to create a gratitude journal. When we take the time to focus on all we are grateful for—we receive even MORE things to be grateful for! Living in gratitude is a wonderful way to elevate our vibrations!

11. DESIRE: By focusing on desire, we automatically raise our frequency level. When we place our attention on our desires we are encouraged to take action and move forward. When we have an approach of apathy, meaning we don't care about anything, we will naturally be in a lower level of vibrations.

12. WORDS: Choose your words mindfully. Choose to be a person who selects words wisely and consciously. Those who do this are the people who show higher respect for themselves and compassion for others. Our words are extremely powerful. What we speak, we think. What we think, we attract. By using only words that are carefully selected and words that stem from a love centered heart, we naturally *feel* better.

13. CONNECT WITH YOUR SOUL: Understand that at your core, you are a spiritual being who has a physical body. If you are at a low vibrating frequency, this may seem unrealistic to you and challenging to understand. As you practice quieting your mind and being mindful of your core, you become better at connecting with your soul-self. Point to yourself. Where did you point? I bet you pointed around your "heart" area. This indicates you know your soul is who you really are. You are not your face—you are indeed—your soul.

14. STEP INTO YOUR FEAR: When we face our fears and step into them, we are able to advance up the vibrational scale. Who would you become if you were able to conquer your fears? How would you feel if you took action and gave that speech, sang that song in front of others, wrote that book, threw that party, jumped out of a perfectly good airplane, lovingly confronted a certain person?

15. FOOD: Being mindful of the food you eat that is personally best for your physical, mental, and spiritual needs are vitally important for elevating and maintaining your vibration level. High Vibrational people eat healthy foods. Many opt for a vegetarian or vegan diet. Low Vibrational people eat processed, junk food and greasy fast food. Choose a healthy plan that makes you feel your best!

16. BREATH: Are you aware of your breathing pattern? Being fully conscious of how you are breathing is important. There is a proper way to breathe that is optimal for your brain and your body of which many are unaware. Optimal breathing involves inhaling through your nose and exhaling through your mouth upon each breath. When we become more aware of breathing in this manner, we reap the benefits of an increased level of focus and stability.

17. BE OPEN-MINDED: Our world has so much to offer in many areas such as different religions, beliefs, cultures, and nature and when we accept the diversity our vibration level skyrockets! We can also be open-minded to try something new such as a new food, spiritual practice, or an exercise routine.

18. BRAIN BOOSTER: Do you ever wonder why you oftentimes see people with Crossword Puzzle magazines or those Find The Word books? Those people have learned activities like these naturally boost their brainpower, which raises their Vibrations!

19. AFFIRMATIONS: Affirmations are used to change beliefs and thinking patterns. For example: "I am strong," "I am healthy," and "I am joyful." Affirmations are used to reprogram our thoughts from beliefs that don't serve our highest good to patterns of thoughts that assist us with living our best life.

20. REACH FOR THE HIGHEST THOUGHT: William James said it best when he declared, *"The Greatest Weapon Against Stress Is Our Ability To Choose One Thought Over Another."* Throughout the day be mindful of your thoughts and how they make you feel. When you have a thought that does not make you feel your best, make a choice to change that thought and reach for the highest thought! With practice, you'll be living with a higher quality of thoughts.

I share *many* ways to raise your vibrations when I present at workshops and perhaps now you have a better idea of what it would be like to spend a full day with me! I often tell my clients, "The most important thing you can do on a daily basis for yourself to live your best life is to focus on raising your vibrations. That's where the good stuff is! What works for you *may or may not* work for your friends or family—and that's okay! Just focus on *you* and not only will *you* benefit but *everyone* around you will too or ... they will move on! I cannot think of anything I would enjoy more than doing what I do ... educating others on how to move themselves up the Vibrational Scale, toward love.

To all those I have been fortunate enough to meet on this journey, I am aware of your magnificent higher-self and I honor you.

Dedicated to my incredible daughter-in-law, Kirstie Myers-Miller. If God would have chosen to bless me with a biological daughter ... I would have wanted her to be exactly like you. Thank you for your love and for being such an extraordinary mother to my granddaughter, Maci Dawn Miller. Also to my loving and supportive family, many amazing friends and the incredibly courageous clients I am fortunate enough to have surrounding me in my life. You bless my life in your own unique way, and I am abundantly grateful for each and every one of you.

~ Lisa Hardwick-Peplow

Lindsley Silagi

LINDSLEY SILAGI, Educator and Professional Coach with a private coaching practice, Step By Step Results!, in Santa Teresa, New Mexico where she lives with her husband, Lon. She conducts healing and motivational workshops and retreats to help others release and let go of lack and limitation, "get into flow," and to connect with their soul's calling.

Lindsley loves dance, art, people, photography, and travel. And most of all she loves to share a great laugh with a friend.

www.stepbystepresults.net

Called To Love

"Why can't we give love one more chance?"

~ FREDDY MERCURY

Are you ready to give LOVE a chance?

What is the impact that you might have if you commit to living from LOVE? What could you do in love and with love that no one else would do? What is yours to love uniquely? How might the challenges that you face today be changed in and through love? I believe we are here and called to love, every one of us. Are you responding to this call? We are called to love in the midst of challenge. We are called to love that which challenges us and our capacity to love. The alternative is not a solution. So the question we must ask ourselves is:

Do I want to be part of the solution? Do I want to be the embodiment of the solution?

If your inner voice responds that it is time to love, *listen*. Pay attention to the call of LOVE. Recognize that love is needed and that it is within each one of us. When you do you place your feet on the pathway to greater success, greater freedom, and greater wholeness.

What Is The Nature Of Love

Probably no other topic in the world has more written about it than LOVE. It is the topic of poetry throughout the ages. It is central to all of the teachings of the great spiritual masters. It is the topic of countless songs. Love is an energy, the source of which all of us can access. We can be loving as well as feel the warmth of being loved. We can expand our love or we can shut it down. When we do the latter, we discover that life loses meaning and we go off course. The Spirit of Love that we have within us is for sharing. Only when we share our love will it grow, expand, and multiply.

Sometimes we learn the most from that which we teach to our children. I have such a teaching to share here. I taught my first grade students many years ago, the song that follows. It is titled, "Love is a Magic Penny," written by Malvina Reynolds in the 1950's. I have included it here for you to read and for you to consider its message. If you happen to know it, sing it aloud. It you do not, try simply reading the words aloud as they have more power this way.

 Love Is A Magic Penny

> *Love is something if you give it away,*
> *give it away, give it away,*
> *Love is something if you give it away,*
> *you end up having more.*
>
> *It's just like a magic penny.*
> *Hold it tight and you won't have any.*
> *Lend it, spend it and you'll have so many*
> *They'll roll all over the floor.*

For

Love is something if you give it away,
give it away, give it away
Love is something if you give it away,
you end up having more.

Money's dandy and we like to use it
But love is better, if you don't refuse it
It's a treasure and you'll never lose it
Unless you lock up your door.

For

Love is something if you give it away,
give it away, give it away
Love is something if you give it away,
you end up having more.

So let's go dancing 'till the break of day
And if there's a piper, we can pay
For love is something if you give it away
You end up having more.

(If you are interested in hearing the original version of this tune sung by Malvina herself it is on You Tube here) http://www.youtube.com/watch?v=FB5Z_30xSe8&feature=youtu.be)

Love is indeed an inside to outside process, one filled with joy.

Probably the best definition of the many aspects of the power we call love comes to us from the following highly quoted verse in the Bible:

Love is patient, love is kind. It does not envy, it does not boast, it is not proud. It is not rude, it is not self-seeking, it is not easily angered, it keeps no record of wrongs. Love does not delight in evil but rejoices with the truth. It always protects, always trusts, always hopes, always perseveres.

~1 CORINTHIANS 13:4-8

If we are to know love as it is defined here and how to experience it more fully in our lives, I have learned that we must be willing to inquire within to discover how to release any blocks. So let's consider how.

The Inquiry

So how do we move into the LOVE energy that is within us? First, we may want to inquire into what we believe about our emotions. Do you believe that you are in charge of your emotions or do you allow your emotions to be in charge of you? There was a time in my life when I was ruled by my emotions. And one day, I realized that my life was not working out the way I had in mind. In fact, it was just the opposite. I was awash in fear, loneliness, worry, and unhappiness. It was then that I began to explore how to make the changes necessary to be in charge of my emotions, and to take greater responsibility for my life, my thinking, and my results. I learned that the way we feel depends largely upon the way we think and upon the beliefs we hold to be true. It is what we believe that gets us tripped up and causes the negative emotions of fear, anger, abandonment, worry. I have learned that the key to shifting out of any of these undesirable emotional states is by challenging them.

One way to do that is to have a little dialogue with yourself.

It might sound like this:

Self to Self: *So are you feeling sad?*

Self: *Yes*

Self to Self: *So how long do you want to feel this sadness?*

Self: *Not long.*

Self to Self: *What emotion would you rather be feeling?*

Self: *Love.*

Self to Self: *Love? Great! How will you experience this?*

Self: *Hmmm. I don't know.*

Self to Self: *First, perhaps you could share this sadness with a trusted friend.*

Self: *Yes, I could do this.*

Self to Self: *Good. Then maybe you could meditate. Maybe this will help you let it go. Maybe you could get out in nature and get a new perspective.*

When we challenge ourselves to shift out of the negative emotion, we take a significant step. It is up to us. When we do our life will transform. Before I knew this I kept coming up against barriers to my happiness. I thought that my happiness was dependent upon my outer experiences being a certain way. When they did not unfold the way I wanted them to unfold, then I would be unhappy. This would cause further unhappiness. It would snowball out of control. Once I learned that happiness was my choice a whole new world opened up for me.

It can for you too.

Are you willing to be changed?

Choose to lay down the need you have inside you to be right. Stop listening to the EGO self and the felt need you think you must fill. This is the need to be right. Ask yourself:

"So just suppose right here, right now that perhaps you are not **'right'**? What if your view of this situation is not **'right'**?" This can be powerful. I encourage you to try it. It can open you up to recognize new perspectives. When we challenge ourselves and learn how to be less judgmental of situations, people, and events we may discover we have the life we wanted all along. It may just be momentary at first. But then we realize that we can create another moment and then another one, and pretty soon we realize we have the life that we always dreamed of, moment by moment.

Once we learn how to get out of the way of our happiness, we find it appears before us. This is through letting go of the judgment and criticism and choosing to listen to and move from the love we have inside of us. We can live in our fear-based outer world or we can choose to create from the loving life force that is given to us. We can choose to live again and to love again no matter the circumstances or situations that we have experienced. We can choose to love every moment of every day. Why would we choose anything less for ourselves, for the ones we love and for our world? It all starts when we choose to make a change in our thoughts.

Remember love is the most prospering power there is. It is within each of us and when we listen, it calls us to be who we really were meant to be. Become willing to inquire within. It will help you to discover any limiting beliefs you may have that need to be released. Here are some questions to move you into this inquiry.

❧ Patience

Do I live life with patience? Or am I impatient all the time? How might I shift this? What is one thing I am willing to do today to change?

❧ Kindness

Do I live life in kindness? Or not? How might I increase my kindness? What might I need to give up in order to do this?

❧ Trust

Do I live in trust? Do I trust others? Do others trust me? How might I increase my trust level?

❧ Perseverance

Am I in it for the short term or the long term? What might I need to do or give up doing to increase my level of perseverance?

On Forgiveness

Forgiveness is a dimension of love that opens us to greater expression of love in our life. It opens us to joy and happiness. But first we must establish a practice of forgiving. Here are some questions for you to ask yourself to begin this process.

Do I have someone I need to forgive?

Do I need to forgive myself?

Do I need to forgive someone in my family?

Am I forgiving of events and experiences of the past?

What about the current events that happen in the blink of an eye each day? Am I willing to let go of the little disappointments that happen?

What do I believe about forgiveness?

Do I think of forgiveness as a weakness?

Do I consider forgiveness a strength?

Who might need my forgiveness now?

What Forgiveness Does

Forgiveness frees you. It frees up your energy. You physically have more energy for the things that you are creating in your life, the projects, family gatherings, your work life. Forgiveness requires that you shift out of a limited belief, one that does not serve you or the world.

Sometimes when people encounter the idea of forgiveness, specifically forgiveness of self, they resist the idea. At first you may feel this too. However, if you are willing to dig deeper you may hear a judgmental voice inside yourself. This judgmental voice criticizes you every time you do what you deem to be a mistake. What mistakes have you made, big or small? Forgive yourself. Forgive yourself for judging yourself harshly. This process helps you to shift into the energy of loving. Love yourself instead of judging yourself. Then love others instead of judging others. Try this out and notice how you feel. The energy of LOVE is healing, calming, soothing. Move into it through the door of forgiveness.

Commitment

Are you ready to commit more to the energy of love? Make a commitment to it. This will open doors for you. Remember this:

There are two basic motivating forces: fear and love. When we are afraid, we pull back from life. When we are in love, we open to all that life has to offer with passion, excitement, and acceptance. We need to learn to love ourselves first, in all our glory and our imperfections. If we cannot love ourselves, we cannot fully open to our ability to love others or our potential to create. Evolution and all hopes for a better world rest in the fearlessness and open-hearted vision of people who embrace life.

~ JOHN LENNON

The stories in this book are offered to inspire you to choose love over fear. Open to love each day. I encourage you to make a commitment to it. Move from this energy consciously. Be kind to yourself and patient in the process. You will make mistakes but love yourself through it. Give yourself credit for the effort you make to shift to a positive perceptive. Just make a decision to do this and then notice how your life changes. It will work for you if you commit to it.

I would like to close this chapter with a quote from Christian D. Larsen that my mother shared with me many years ago. My mother has always endeavored to live from this positive outlook and inspired me to live from this sunny perspective too. It is my hope that I will continue to live into its vision. And now I hope that you will too.

Promise Yourself

 Promise yourself to be so strong that nothing can disturb your peace of mind. Look at the sunny side of everything and make your optimism come true. Think only of the best, work only for the best, and expect only the best. Forget the mistakes of the past and press on to the greater achievements of the future. Give so much time to the improvement of yourself that you have no time to criticize others. Live in the faith that the whole world is on your side so long as you are true to the best that is in you!

~ CHRISTIAN D. LARSON

Thank you to all who have touched my life.

You do know who you are.

And because of you I know myself more fully.

To my Mom

who taught me

about Love.

~ Lindsley Silagi

Verity Dawson

VERITY DAWSON is a well-traveled citizen of the world, now settled in Barbados. She is highly respected on-island and has appeared on TV and radio and speaks to groups on the mind/body/spirit unit throughout the Caribbean.

Originally finding fulfillment through the UN/World Food Programme, she then switched gears to an energy healing practice, creating the first 'new age' bookstore in Barbados. She combines the Heal Your Life® principles as a licensed Coach and Workshop leader with a traditional guidance and counseling training.

www.CaribHolisticInsights.com

A Journey

I hail from a nomadic lifestyle - one Grandpa was a ship's engineer, the other a superintendent on the railways, both in India.

Long journeys going one way or t' other from India to England, the HomeLand, involved water; but local travel, in the days prior to accessible air travel, were always by train. So that is the metaphor I use for this sharing my move toward love with you, dear reader.

> "...what thrills me about trains is not their size or their equipment but that they are moving, that they embody a connection between unseen places."
>
> ~ MARIANNE WIGGINS

There have been plenty of stops. At many stations, I actually felt like I might have reached my destination; but no, my old-fashioned transport is still clickety-clacking along the rails and sometimes even runs into patches of smooth newly-laid tracks designed for a quiet ride. Coal has been replaced by electricity and I dare say, being environmentally conscious, I might switch to a magnetic impulse mono-rail shortly. Grandpa Dawson's large gold fob watch, fabled to bring the Dawson train precisely on time to its destination, now has both hands stopped at noon or midnight, with the second hand fallen to the bottom of the case. This may explain the anomaly of any journey. You could be 12 hours out at any point ... halfway arrived, or half a day late. Glass half full or glass half empty. Unless of course you go digital. We certainly seem to have more choices in this day and age.

What I do remember is being stopped on a track, in the middle of one journey upcountry to visit relatives, in the dead of night, with beasts and other wildlife prowling with intent to see what was on offer in the way of a meal on wheels. Myself and a Grandma, she staying the nerves and re-assuring little Me that we were protected in our compartment. Both Grandmas psychic and encouraging me by their example to remember that we were not just flesh and to sense what else was going on "out there". I saw too much and was more than terrified. Harry Potter's Hogwarts castle of magic was no comparison to what my imagination could create.

The Journey

I recall one early momentous stop of my actual Soul Journey. The train stayed at the station long enough for me to digest the birth of my first beautiful daughter. On seeing her unique, albeit jaundiced face, my heart swelled to the point that I now recognise was pure ecstasy. What an experience for a young girl such as myself, who had lived an isolated life in remote areas and frequently been the only child in the community, to now hold this fragile being in my arms. It made my life come alive in ways I could not even begin to anticipate.

Second Major Stop

And then there was an equally crucial stop two and a half years later - the birth of my second daughter. How could I, undeserving as I was, be privy to cherish yet another small being, so attached to me, whose eyes followed my every move and whose best place in the world was to nestle near my heart.

I took both those experiences and placed them on the overhead rack in my carriage and lovingly cared for them even as I wrestled with the poor conditions in the cabin as the train rocked noisily and we hurtled along. No known destination at this point.

The carriage careened through long dark tunnels of never-ending depression and confusion and rushed violently over precarious arches hung like fine cobwebs over scary abyss, when any movement, any wrong word, might have sent all plummeting into oblivion. I still clung to my seat with a deep inner conviction that I could not be on this journey without a reason, with a feeling lodged within my core that I was on this ride for a significant purpose. Not just to nurture my two precious children to a meaningful existence, but lurking somewhere in the baggage compartment an important package presented upon departure and, as yet, unopened. It never left my mind and it called strongly for attention.

Finally, that train slid to a sickening halt in an unexpected siding and I trekked my precious cargo in a blurry fog back to a family station. I picked up the package and glanced at the label - Guidelines: Being Of Service to People and the Planet. Who could be bothered with that right at this moment of needing to identify a sleeker, smoother passenger train?

I choose to be me became my heart's cry. I had to be authentic. I did not know what an affirmation was then, but this unsung and deeply intuitive mantra guided my journey in this second phase. Even though I trod very cautiously, I nonetheless explored every minute possibility which this affirmation demanded of me. It included being part of the UN/World Food Programme, learning social as well as professional skills, enhancing my knowledge of what was current in the still developing world and showed me that I had possibilities well beyond anything I could have imagined.

Sustenance

By the time when hunger became apparent, food began to be served on this new train.

One hors d'oevres offered actually turned out to be a feast which has lasted many years and from which I can still nibble a morsel or two now and again. The menu stated: A Course In Miracles (ACIM). The menu explained this item: it told me that I was a miracle worker, that God loved me - no matter what. That I could choose to take off my glasses and look at Life, really look at Life, in a different way. That when I forgave myself, it would be easy to forgive others. I took it all on board and channelled love at every opportunity. There was no one who could escape my eyes consciously radiating Light connected to some point above my crown (no pun intended!), no mood which could deter me as I paced the train looking for opportunities to anchor this new thinking.

Becoming curiouser and more curiouser than an Alice In Wonderland, I finally determined to open the package stored in the baggage compartment. Imagine my shock to recognise that I had already been operating on the guidelines contained in the paperwork in this suitcase. I had found my dharma. I was on the right track!

Turning Point

One station I rested awhile was in a bookstore in which Spirit helped me to create. A book by Marsha Sinetar - Do What You Love and The Money Will Follow - was the inspiration. What did I love to do? Read. How could that become my Doing? Easy. Barbados, where I now lived, had no new age centre and my bookstore became a hub for those thirsty for knowledge and fresh ways of living.

One day a young overseas visitor came into the store. She was small, plump and nervous, tension oozed out of her. Attitude was immediately recognisable. My heart sank. Here was trouble. But no, I remembered that I always had a choice! I could look at this differently - I could choose to channel Love.

 Clean but the mirror and the message shines forth

~ A COURSE IN MIRACLES

Here instead was a Christ. I could welcome this manifestation of a Chip Off The Old Block and in the flick of the wrist, my Love Eyes consciously switched to High Beam. Love was in the air. It was irresistible. In no more than 20 minutes, this woman shape-shifted into the softest person you could imagine. Her shoulders dropped, her mouth took on a smile and she confided that she was quite stressed out from promoting woman's gay liberation through a black movement in what might be called an emancipated country. We became friends. Sat down and had a coffee on the house (yes, I had thought of that long before the famous bookstores adopted the policy!) and found that we in fact we had so much in common. We promised to meet up when I had an overseas stop, and we did indeed connect at a station cafe briefly to update the story of each other's journey.

Last course

The dessert served on the travelling food wagon, delivered by an efficient waitering service determined to waste no time in digestion after the ACIM main meal, was *You Can Heal Your Life*. This book written by Louise L. Hay, had been carefully lowered onto my placemat and I delved greedily into every word. Louise Hay, my friend, my mentor, my role model, guided me into introspection, again re-iterated me to love myself, explained that bodily symptoms were just indicators of how and where I had stopped loving myself enough, thoughts were things, and I had the Power Within Me. She became my role model and I started a second Move Toward Love. The injunctions contained in my opened package now began to take on a different meaning. My vision grew higher, the inner yearnings to be of service wanted to touch every soul I could reach.

Imagine my bliss when I met her some years later to learn that she was also a wise woman, worldly, with a great sense of humour. Those periodic stops in the early years of the Heal Your Life® teacher trainings where I was privileged to assist, were very special.

Forgiveness

On my train, I bumped into a conductor floating along the corridors. She not only checked the tickets - she was giving them out! This beautiful generous soul was none other than Dr. Patricia Crane. She had been mentored by Louise Hay and had taken on the mantle of spreading Louise Hay's message. She taught me by example once again about forgiveness, giving the benefit of the doubt, looking on every landscape we passed, fair or foul, as another opportunity to enjoy the journey. I could not have had a more poignant reminder of why I was on this train.

The continuation

 "It is good to have an end to journey toward, but it is the journey that matters in the end."

~ URSULA K. LE GUIN

Once you are on this Journey, there is actually no end. Love - which you thought was the destination - actually turns out to be the stuff of the journey.

What is the strategy, I hear you ask? Just channel love? How do you move toward love?

Past the days of seeing a Christ, I now use compassion. I think and see this person as a frightened and confused little child. S/he is in a situation where the ground feels slippery and the rules seem to change moment by moment. What this child is asking for is simply to be hugged, to be loved and accepted - no matter what. When I can recognise that, I can also recognise my little inner child and her tremblings. Compassion becomes automatic. I do not have to look for it. I do not have to strain for it. I do not have to judge the situation.

I believe we have all chosen a Journey. You may be using the fast lane - taking personal development workshops and jetting straight to the next stop. Or perhaps you have decided on cruising, taking time to read, digest, working your way into community projects.

Just know this interesting fact: when a plane travels from Point A to Point B, it is only on course 10%, yes 10% - of the journey. In the pioneer days of aviation, the flight navigator had his small space near the cockpit and would keep rectifying the course with a compass so that the plane arrived where it was supposed to, on time. Nowadays, the computer does it all but the pilot still takes conscious decisions over and above the information and recommendations being provided. So even if you are on board a ship, the captain may very well choose to tack and thus you appear to be going backwards rather than forwards, and that is OK. Whatever your mode of transport ... know that, rather like the planets, there will be moments of apparent retrograde, but that is only an illusion - the Universe is still spinning its way into Eternity.

"Why does every road eventually narrow into a point at the horizon? Because that's where the point lies."

~ VERA NAZARIAN,

THE PERPETUAL CALENDAR OF INSPIRATION

Conclusion

I have travelled far and wide, in every sense of the word. We may be on the same train, sharing a carriage for any stage of the trip, or in a different cabin but headed in the same direction. We may be on different tracks, passing strangers in the night or sometimes speeding at the same rate and making eye contact into a lighted window, sharing a knowing look. Mostly the face we see in the window is but a self-reflection. I hope my Journey can be of service to you in reminding you that we are all on different tracks, passing strangers in the night, sometimes looking from window to window as our trains take the same speed. Those moments of connection are the fabric that binds our Universe in a matrix of inter-dependence.

Thank you for sharing the ride with me.

 "Love is the only answer to every question. It is the only thing that will serve you in every situation. It is the route and the destination. It is medication, liberation and should be at the heart of and expression of your vocation."

~ RASHEED OGUNLA

Thanks and much gratitude for the many teachers and innovators on my Journey. In particular, Dr. Patricia Crane for her solid friendship and for providing me incredible opportunities to fulfil my life purpose; to Rick Nichols for his loving friendship, humour and wisdom; to Michael Ryce for making A Course In Miracles come alive as a way of life; to Louise Hay for her gracious hospitality to all the early Heal Your Life® newbies and for inspiring humanity to open its heart chakra; and to my dear friend Denise Carrs, whose loyalty and love supported me through the dark times.

Dedicated to my daughters, Justine and Jessica, who provided me such rich living experiences and who prompted me to keep learning more, so to share thoughts, ideas and knowledge with them; to my father for providing a philosophical framework to live by; and my mother for her unconditional loving support.

~ Verity Dawson

Jim Mills

JIM MILLS has worked in California agriculture for over thirty years. He currently advises farmers, growers and ranchers on sustainable crop nutrition programs and responsible nutrient management. Jim delights in spreading seeds of consciousness, and inspiring others to step into their Infinite potency to create a life and living that works for them, free of judgment and full of possibility and choice.

The father of four adult sons, he resides in Morro Bay, California and enjoys exploring the valleys, hills and beaches of the Central Coast.

jim@jimmymills805.com
www.jimmymills805.com
http://facebook.com/jimmy.mills.805

Remembering And Returning To The Love Within

 Love your neighbor as yourself.

~ JESUS

Beautiful words, and I am seeing them with new awareness. You see, I have always focused on the first part of the verse, completely missing the potency and possibility hidden in the second. This is not a story about loving your neighbor, but please practice more of that! It makes the world go 'round! This is a story about loving oneself. It is a celebration of one man's journey, my journey, back to the love within. Divine love. Human love. Self love. Love that permeates and infuses every molecule of one's being, and contains the potency to transform everything it touches. I've heard of the ancient traditions of the warrior-poets. Perhaps I am that, but this I know with certainty, I am a lover-poet. The essence of my being, and the energy of my life and living is love, in all of its magnificent expressions! Love is what I choose. A lover is who I be. Love is both my soul focus, and my sole desire. Choose love. Be love.

Tapping Into The Love Within

I am fully human, with two feet firmly planted on Mother Earth. I have the joy and privilege of working in agriculture, contributing to a vast array of fruits, vegetable, grains and nuts, facilitating them in bringing forth the abundant harvest they desire to gift the planet. Every cell in creation has consciousness bursting within, and these are no exception. It brings me great happiness to walk through an almond orchard, vineyard, or strawberry field and be still and listen. Just listen, and ask how I might contribute to their grandest expression of themselves. It is very grounding having one's hands or feet under the skin of Mother Earth, touching her insides. I find the Divine here. I find infinite possibility here. I find love here.

I have been married twice to brilliant and gifted women whom I adore, and we chose to bring both marriages to an end. Four sweet sons were birthed into the world through us, and we continue to marvel at the young men they are choosing to be. I've enjoyed success in business, and been honored for civic contribution. I have also grappled with addictive behavior, watched a business I created crash and burn, and publicly endured the shame and embarrassment of repossession, foreclosure and bankruptcy. On a soul level, I now know I created all this, fully and completely. Experiences that I thought would surely crush and destroy me have instead become the greatest gifts I have ever allowed myself to receive. They have been the doorway through which I wrestled with myself and the Universe, writhed in the darkness of agony and despair, and ultimately emerged from the flames a more conscious, aware and loving man. The words of Lao Tzu resonate with me: "New beginnings are often disguised as painful endings." I found the Divine here. I found love here. I found Jim here! I also know that none of these experiences, the successes or the failures, define who I am today. They are just choices, and I am free to choose again, in limitless present moment possibility.

You don't have a Soul. You are a Soul. You have
a body.

~ C. S. LEWIS

I have such a knowing that I am an infinite being who has chosen to come and play in this magnificent and gifting human frame, and embody an ever expanding expression of love and infinite possibility. This is what excites me, and this is the energy, space and consciousness from which my life flows. It is all love, fully human and fully divine. It is in love that I find my purpose for being, and my contribution to Oneness. What potent creators we are! As infinite beings, what if the only limitations that exist are the ones we make solid, significant and real? My great joy is infusing infinite energy and possibility into the human experience, busting asunder the perceived limitations of this reality, and moment by moment creating a life and living far richer, fuller and fun than I ever imagined possible! Choosing to be love feels light and filled with ease, because it is the source from which I came. It is nurturing and refreshing, and full of happiness and smiles! It began as a conscious choice, and it continues to expand and flow as the essence and creative energy of my life and living. Everything I desire resides in love. Everything I require resides in love. I choose to be love, and receive love, and gift love to myself and others, to Infinite Yummy (my playful and affectionate name for Source!), and to all of creation. I can imagine no higher calling or grander vocation.

 We become what we think about all day long.

~ RALPH WALDO EMERSON

Being Our Unique Expression Of Love

I've ceased trying to define love. I simply choose to flow in the energy of it. Love is infinite. Love is limitless. How can that which is infinite be defined? Any attempt to do so by definition results in limitation, and there is no limitation in love. As the song declares "Love is a many splendored thing." The expressions of love are infinite, and the world is full of beautiful works of word, song, and artistic creation reflecting the many faces and expressions of love. In its essence, love transcends definition. I choose to be love, and allow it to ooze and drip from my being as honey oozes and drips from a gorged honeycomb, covering everything it touches with its sticky sweet goodness!

 To love oneself is the beginning of a lifelong romance.

~ OSCAR WILDE

I first married at twenty-one years of age, and I was totally unprepared for what would follow. We both discovered early on that my communication skills were virtually non-existent. It would drive my fiery Irish American bride to fits of rage, and I remember her coming into the bedroom pouring glasses of water on my head in her frustration. Needless to say, this did nothing to help me open up, and I despised her in those moments. We stayed married for fourteen years, in part because I could not comprehend the concept of ending a marriage. Both our parents were still married! Today, twenty-four years after the divorce, we laugh about it and are dear and supportive friends, and she recently stayed an evening in my home on her way from Napa to San Diego to visit our third born son.

After the divorce, it was only a matter of months before I started jumping into a series of relationships. Spending time alone was a foreign concept, and I hadn't yet awakened to the possibility of going within and nurturing my inner being. I truly enjoyed this time in my life, spending time with my three young sons and jumping in and out of a series of short relationships with fun and interesting women. Five years passed, and I met and married a kind and loving woman, who became an instant and loving step-mom to my three young boys, and a year later gave birth to another beautiful son, now eighteen years of age. We enjoyed many happy moments, and she stood by me support- ively during the massive financial collapse that shook our personal world in 2007. Despite all this, there were core areas where we were not compatible, and it left me feeling separate, alone and empty. I was craving a level of connection that was not present in our relationship. I would judge myself harshly and make myself wrong for my inability to be happy in our marriage. I had a wife who was loving and support- ive. Why wasn't that enough? Why did I feel so unhappy and alone? It became unbearable, and in January 2011, after seeing the film "Eat, Pray, Love," and reading Elizabeth Gilbert's next book "Committed: A Love Story" in one sitting, I asked my wife for a divorce ... via text message while she was out of town with friends. What a prince of a guy! I'm not proud of how I communicated this desire, and wish I had waited to have this conversation face to face, but I was sick of feeling alone in the marriage, and I could not wait another second to start being true to myself. And so we brought our marriage of sixteen years to a conclusion, with minimal rancor and the scorched earth mentality that so often defines the divorce process. My intention from the day we separated was to model a way to exit a marriage that honors each of our paths, the time we chose to spend together, and the man child that came into the world through us. Yes, there were trying moments, and I am proud of how we conducted ourselves. I often reflect on my choice to exit the marriage. Outwardly, it appears to be such a judgable offense. Inwardly, only I know my heart and what is true for me, and I simply had to honor that without regard for the judgments of others.

This is the path to peace, and the possibility of living a more authentic and happy life. My heart and voice finds refuge and strength in the mantra of the Hawaiian healing system known as Ho'oponopono: "I'm sorry, please forgive me, thank you, I love you." I meditate and voice this potent expression throughout the day. I offer it to the Divine, and to all those in my life.

Ok, Hot Shot, You Asked For It, Now What?

For the first time in thirty-five years I was living by myself. Actually, for the first time in *my entire life* I was truly living by myself. Mind you, I had no great desire to live alone, quite the contrary. I thrive on intimate loving connection. I assumed I would find a loving partner, my soulmate, in short order and begin a new chapter in my life. I was correct in one regard, a new chapter had begun, it just looked different than I expected! My higher self, and love itself, began drawing me on a journey within ... a returning to me. A journey of remembering the love I be, and I am so very grateful.

The past three years have been both the most rewarding, and the most challenging of my life. It has been a time of self reflection, forgiveness, and opening my heart to love and new beginnings. I have been brought face to face with all of me, or at least as much as I am able to see and receive, and I have been able to acknowledge that I was the common denominator in both marriages and every relationship throughout my life that I chose to walk away from. My sense of separation and aloneness was rooted deep in my being, and not some real or perceived shortcoming in my partner. I discovered, at a deep level, that I did not know how to love and nurture myself. I did not know how to gift myself the same kindness and compassion that I was willing to give to others. I discovered a vast cauldron of self judgment and self loathing, and I knew that in facing it I was doing the most important work of my life. I embraced the process, and settled in for what might prove to be a long solo ride, perhaps a lifelong journey remembering how to both like and love me, and finding happiness living with me. Forgiving myself, and letting go of self judgment has become a daily practice. Choosing to embrace and love me, and inviting infinite love to be the energy and consciousness of my life and living is generative and transformational beyond my greatest imaginings!

 Our humanity is the portal to our divinity.

~ PANACHE DESAI

Daily Practice

The afternoon of life is such a delightful time. Youthful ambition and outward focus on accumulating more stuff has faded, and life and living is characterized by a sense of purpose, meaning, and service. Choosing what nurtures and brings happiness has new value. Connecting deeply with Source through meditation and being in nature brings great joy and contentment. I am discovering that loving and nurturing self is a required discipline for a happy life, and a daily practice. I take time for me, doing what brings happiness and contributes to my sense of balance. I find time to be in nature most every day, and have become an avid walker. Some might call it power walking, while I choose to call it 'energy walking.' I love to be in nature along ocean's edge, country valley or mountain trail and feel connected with the Source energy inherent in nature. It has become my daily practice, a time and place to meditate, reflect and connect in a deep way with my higher self and Infinite Yummy. It is a time of creation and infinite possibility and my creative energies surge and find expression and direction on my walks. My mp3 player is loaded with scores of inspirational and transforma-tional lectures, interviews and music by a multitude of mentors whose contribution I cherish and value. Often I put in my ear buds, listen for an hour or so, and then walk back in solitude and quiet reflection.

I've also rediscovered my love of gardening. I love all flowers and plants, and delight in planting, watering and watching them grow and erupt in a masterpiece of color, texture and beauty! I thank my sweet mother for this, and the garden is a place where I connect with her energy and beingness, and the simple and happy memories of a loving mother and son. I am constantly showing people I meet pictures of my flower garden, it brings me such happiness. It is so rewarding to see honey-bees, butterflies and hummingbirds flitting around the yard. Even the spiders are welcome!

About eighteen months ago I broke a bone in my left foot while I was ... walking! Are you kidding me?! I was devastated. I had to wear a remov-able boot and attempt to stay off it for what seemed like an eternity. Not being able to take my daily walks was a major blow to my psyche. What's right about this that I'm not getting? All of a sudden I'm pretty much house bound. Yikes! I've always been a voracious reader, so I took advantage of the sedentary time to enjoy a variety of books to nurture both my soul and my mind. I also rediscovered the simple pleasure of being in the kitchen and the joy of creating delicious meals. Living in coastal California offers a seemingly endless cornucopia of fresh fruits, vegetables and seafood, and I enjoy them all! My little cottage has limited counter space, and I decided I needed a larger more functional prep area where two people could stand and work facing one another. I found an old desk at an antique emporium down the street and brought it home. A fresh coat of paint, new drawer hardware, a set of casters and a glass top and boom --- a functional kitchen island that rolls wherever its needed, and most importantly allows two people the space to create both yummy food and great conversation together!

Losing the ability to exercise, and rediscovering the joy of cooking is a problematic combination! I've become much more sensitive to what my body desires and requires. I live in a state of constant amazement at how gifting my body is, and the unconditional love it has always extended to me, even in the midst of destructive behaviors that I chose to inflict upon it. It has always been here for me, and I'm learning to listen to it, sense its feather touch of awareness, and honor and facilitate it in what it desires. My body clearly offered awareness that it desired a different shape and size than that which I had been forcing on it, and in four months time I joyfully facilitated it in releasing twenty-five pounds with ease! It has been twenty years since my body has visited this size and weight. It feels great! I feel great!

And so my life and living continues to blossom, transform and expand. I've become my own best friend, my own soulmate. I enjoy my own company, and trust my knowing and intuition. In this space of love, beautiful friends are showing up in my life, and I am grateful. Gifting kindness, compassion and love to oneself creates the space to develop loving and generative relationships with those who show up in our life. This is the practice of "Love your neighbor as yourself." Each day is a new opportunity to engage in the deliberate creation of our life and living. What are the possibilities when we choose to be happy, and surround ourselves with that which brings us joy? Life becomes a wondrous and whimsical playground to explore with childlike curiosity and appreciation. I choose to be love, and love is what I see reflected back to me at every turn. How about you? I Love You.

Appreciation to Mary, Edmond and Stephanie—your love and knowing sustained and guided me to discover the greatness within myself. You continue to be an inspiration, and my heart overflows with thanksgiving for the gift you are to my life and living, and to the planet. I love you.

Dedicated to the Oneness we all truly be, and for the joy and happiness that is ours as we enjoy this dance of life together in beautiful human form.

~ Jim Mills

You will recognize your
own path when you come
upon it because you will
suddenly have all the
energy and imagination
you will ever need.

~ ZIG ZIGLAR

Jennifer Hamende

JENNIFER HAMENDE is a Certified Reiki Master, Certified Mind, Body, Spirit Practitioner, Certified Himalayan Singing Bowl Sound Therapist, and owner of *Winds for Change Healing Center* in Fargo, ND. She has also studied in the fields of Sociology and Gerontology. Ironically, Jennifer's personal story is all about moving toward love and navigating the winds for change. Jennifer attributes being presented with the opportunity to co-author this book to divine timing.

As you read her story, you will witness Jennifer's own spiritual journey through self-discovery, healing, and gratitude as she continues to *move toward love*.

www.windsforchangellc.com
www.jennhamende.com

❦ Winds For Change

Does Spirit talk to you? Most importantly are you open and willing to receive the message being sent to you? Spirit is always trying to communicate with us; sometimes the messages are soft and subtle while other times they are loud and obvious. You never know when messages from Spirit will show up, and if you are not connected to Spirit you may be missing important messages that are being sent to you. I received a Divine message from Spirit while I was visiting a rock shop in Salt Lake City. Hanging on a wall was a sign that read, "Sometimes when faced with the winds for change we find our true direction." The message on the sign was two-fold; first it validated the name *Winds for Change*, which ironically was the name I had recently chosen for the healing center I was opening up, and second, I chose the name *Winds for Change* because I wanted the name to be an extension of my own personal journey. The phrase *Winds for Change* symbolizes an opportunity to turn negative adversities into positive experiences. Spirit continues to guide me to people who are inspirational; they have taught me about self-love, forgiveness, the importance of community, as well as releasing old negative thought patterns that keep me from my true innate self—to be a healer of oneness.

Changing Winds

My belief is that when we experience adverse events in our lives they happen for a reason; each hurdle provides us an opportunity for personal growth. I call these events "teachable moments." It is very important to be open and willing to look at these experiences from another perspective. I realized the less I fed the fear that surrounded my thought process the easier it is to climb out of the pit of hell that I had created for myself, I did this by raising the vibrational energy around me. My journey to spiritual enlightenment has shown me that I no longer have to be defined by my stories in a negative capacity; they are just a part of the journey. We can redefine our stories by positive thoughts, words, and deeds—after all I did choose these experiences when I came into this physical body. I truly believe when faced with winds for change we find our true direction. I am being called to be of service to others so they too may re-discover their true selves and the innate gifts they hold.

 TEACHABLE MOMENT: I am capable of turning adversities into abundance and I need to heal myself so I can be of service to myself and others.

AUGUST 2012: The topic of a healing center came up during a conversation with some good friends of mine. We were discussing how our city would really benefit from a healing center as there are so many of us seeking spiritual growth and community. Long story short, one Friday morning I awoke to a booming voice that said, "Get off your ass and do it"; Spirit sure knows how to get a person's attention. Immediately I phoned a friend and shared with her the message I received. Her response was, "You better get off your ass and do it then!" My journey to find a place for a healing center had begun. While I was looking for a place I found myself struggling to come up with a name for the healing center—it needed to speak to the community as well as my own personal journey.

TEACHABLE MOMENT: Patience - the right space as well as the right name will come with divine timing.

SEPTEMBER 2012: My friend and I attended Sunny Dawn Johnston's Healing Retreat in Flagstaff, Arizona. During this retreat I did a lot of journaling as a desperate act in hopes of finding me among the mess I had created for myself. Awarenesses were an amazing piece of my healing journey despite the pain and resistance that surrounded it.

 TEACHABLE MOMENT: I did not truly love myself and I am a chronic fixer. My need to help and fix others was my coping mechanism to avoid fixing my own issues.

That's My Story And I Am Sticking To It (Or Am I?)

Everyone has a story; I am no exception to the rule. I love sharing my stories—the good and the bad, as well as the ugly. We collect stories throughout the course of our lifetime from conception to death. Our stories are triggered by events that leave positive and negative impacts on our lives. Our ability to get stuck in our story depends on where a person is energetically. Most of my stories were fear based, which resonates at very low vibration energy. For as long as I can remember, I have always felt that I had something to prove to the world and I was put on this earth to accomplish many great things but my choices keep getting in the way. I constantly second guess myself and look to others for approval and validation. Fear is such a powerful and emotional word and I believe that fear has kept me stuck in what I call the merry-go-round effect since the day I was born. During my healing journey I discovered that behind all the facades was a scared little baby who believed that she was not good enough and that she did not fit in.

NOVEMBER 2012: I had an eye opening experience on perception of one's self when a friend introduced me to the Emotional Freedom Technique (EFT). This technique is also known as muscle testing or applied kinesiology. During my EFT session I discovered that my perception of myself became skewed around a particular event—my birth. After testing many scenarios we finally came up with the answer—because of my advanced gestational age, my birth was far from normal. I was born with Meconium Aspiration Syndrome (MAS), which is a complication that occurs when a mother carries the fetus past the 40 week gestational period and the meconium obstructs the airway, and suffocation occurs. I believe I was fully aware of my surroundings when I was born—the sense of urgency, my mother's reaction, as well as the reaction of the hospital staff left such a negative impact on me that my perception of myself became skewed—a sense of fear was instilled in me minutes after my birth. The more we talked about the events that surrounded my birth, the more I was able to uncover the feelings I had been holding onto for 46 years—fear of being scared, different, and not normal. Somehow I did not fit into my family. A major piece of my puzzle was discovered. It was my own fear that fed my perception and was affecting my ability to fit in. Social demands continued to feed into my already fragile state of mind and I became a perfect breeding ground for negative energy. The older I got, fear, shame, and guilt reared its ugly head and I became very critical of myself and I felt as though I didn't fit into my family.

My Story Continues......Perception (Who Is To Blame)

I have always been referred to as the "dreamer" in my family. I lived my life in what some people would call "fairyland" and I felt more alive and safe in that world than in the world I was born into. As a child I had endless conversations with the man on the moon; I shared my joys, fears, as well as my deepest darkest secrets. Even though I had family and friends, I felt very alone. I was in so much pain on the inside that my physical body began to manifest real physical pain(s).

Unconsciously, I became an excellent manifestor at a very young age; however, not in a positive nor productive way. My negative thought patterns were keeping me in a place of low vibrational energy. I started manifesting negative behaviors (drug addiction, promiscuous sexual behaviors, being in an abusive marriage) as well as illnesses (migraine headaches, cysts on my ovaries, severe leg cramps, rheumatoid arthritis) because of the dis-ease within myself. My stories and thought processes kept me at this low vibration and therefore I endured years of pain and suffering. For a while, the famous line "if only" became another significant piece of my story. I even went so far as to blame my parents for my unhappiness; my life was ruined because of the choices they made. To my surprise I could no longer blame others when I learned that the real person responsible for the things that were happening in my life was me. Instead of learning to protect my power, I had learned how to give it away, because I perceived that I was not enough and I did not deserve anything better. Where did my negative self-perception come from? FEAR!

 TEACHABLE MOMENT: I allowed fear to control every aspect of my life; it skewed my perception of life and therefore I created a negative self-image. I am in control of my life I no longer need to blame others for choices in my life. I have the power to keep feeding the fear or move my life toward love. I choose Love!

I Am My Own Teacher

JANUARY 2013: I found myself drawn to attend another class from Sunny Dawn Johnston; this time it was a five day intensive certified Mind, Body, Spirit (MBS) practitioner course. Sunny's MBS course really opened me up and allowed me to take a closer look at whom I really was and who I was pretending to be. As part of the course work, we had to write a letter to ourselves from our body. The following is the letter I wrote:

Dear Jenn,

I have seen you through many, many situations; our body is getting tired of supporting you. It takes two to exchange energy within this body and for more years than I can count I have been doing all the giving and not receiving much back. I am getting tired and worn out and I don't know how much longer I am going to be able to keep supporting you. I need your help!

I have sent you many messages that energy flows better when we work together and for some reason you feel that you have all the power to take all the energy and not replace it. There is no equal exchange of energy. I give, you take. What kind of partnership is this?

Your solution to your blockages is to just cut them out of us. Do you not know what you are doing to us? You're slowly killing us. All you need to do is to speak kindly to us, feed us good food, and move this body; this would show me love. Let others live their life and just concentrate on healing and taking care of us.

I promise I will keep doing my job but I can't do it alone. We came into this life together with a reason, the rate we are going we will not be able to continue to carry out our soul's purpose. So, for you, me, and the Greater Good of the Universe please pay attention to us. Don't worry about what happened in the past you have stressed out our body long enough, focus on the now, so we can have a future.

I would have thought that the messages I have sent you just in the last year alone would have gotten your attention: possible cancer of the eye, gallbladder, breast, and abdomen, lesions on the brain. We can't even enjoy sex because of vaginal dryness and we are full of scar tissue.

You have given me nothing but selfish prayers, medication, and surgery. You can cut the parts of me: gallbladder, all your female parts that is trying to get your attention but this will not stop me from continuing to raise your level of awareness. How did you like the last curveball that I sent you, we were having liver problems; now we are having problems with our blood. I hope you hear this message loud and clear.

I have sent you another cancer scare. I am throwing you a life line are you going to take it and make us better or are you going to throw in the towel once again, it's up to you!

Love Your Body

 TEACHABLE MOMENT: It is really hard to deny the things we do to ourselves when you see them in writing. Being open to the experience has allowed me to take my challenges as an opportunity to see my life from another perspective.

Change Is On Its Way

JANUARY 2013: When I decided to attend Sunny's MBS class in Glendale, Arizona, my husband John and I decided that we would drive to Arizona and spend some quality time together while we were on the road. John travels a lot for his work, so our time together is very limited. I don't like to drive long distances in the car—I am the kind of gal that wants to hop on a plane and just get there. I also suffer from what some people would call "control issues." I decided to take this opportunity to test myself and see how far I had come on my spiritual journey. Could I really get in a car with my hubby and my puppies and drive halfway across the U.S. without much of a plan? I threw caution to the wind and off we went, with the only requirement being I needed to be in Glendale the day before my class started. Let me remind you, we were traveling with two dogs and we had no reservations to speak of; however, we did plan a tentative route. I had to retrain my thought patterns; I kept telling myself, "If I have no expectations I will not be disappointed." I decided to "Let go, let God." It was the best trip I have ever been on. John really seemed interested in what I was learning and we talked every night when I got home from class. I found myself more open and ready to receive—gratitude became my new attitude.

So with my new spiritual awareness in hand, we loaded up the pups in search of our next adventure. While visiting the Petrified Forest, I encountered my first raven; it was so beautiful and majestic—we just sat there staring at each other. I was so in the moment and so aware of my surroundings. As I was reading the signs in the park, I realized each of them contained messages for me: Whispers from the Past, Blue Badlands, Blue Mesa Trail, People and Change, The Changing World, Agate Bridge, From Wood to Stone, The Crystal Forest.

There were other sign names in the park, but to be honest I could not tell you what they were because what happened to me next was one of the most amazing experiences that had ever happened in my life. The pups and I waited in the car while John took a hike along one of the trails. There were two ravens sitting on the post right next to our truck. The puppies were barking, but the ravens were not fazed by their actions—they were staring at me and I at them. I found myself so enthralled by their grace and beauty, I could not help myself—I started to converse with them. The one raven decided to fly away, but the other continued to sit there until all of a sudden it flew away, circled around, and came right back to the same spot. What I witnessed next will stay with me for a lifetime, the raven began to hop and caw to all four directions of the wind. When John got back in the car I excitedly shared with him what I had just witnessed, and when we were about to move to the next spot in the park the other raven came back and sat next to its friend. I had my windows opened so I yelled out at them "Come on girls—let's go to the next spot!" Lo and behold, they started flying above our truck, and when we pulled over to the next spot they stopped with us.

Once again we pulled out to head to the next stop, and once again I yelled out "Come on girls—let's go to the next spot," and once again they were following us. John and I were in complete awe at what happened next—the ravens kept flying right in front of our truck and they would veer to the right and they repeated this pattern a couple of times. We took it as a sign that we needed to pull over. There we witnessed the ravens dancing on top of a sign. They would land, hop up and down a few times, then jump up in the air and land back on the sign. They did this same pattern three times. We were so astonished at what we were witnessing that we forgot to take a picture of the sign or even read it. I have often wondered since then what the sign they were dancing on read (it was probably Winds for Change).

 TEACHABLE MOMENT: "Let go, let God," and when I am in the moment wonderful things are revealed to me.

Releasing What Is No Longer In My Best Interest

APRIL 2013: I was planning on attending another healing retreat with Sunny Dawn Johnston in Sedona, Arizona, but Mother Nature decided to throw a wrench in my plan—Fargo was under severe flood warnings. I only live five blocks from the river and I was a little nervous to say the least. I really teetered back and forth on if I should I stay or go. I decided that I would leave this one up to God. If it didn't flood and Sunny still had an opening I would go (or so I thought). Easter morning I was in my kitchen listening to a few of my favorite cd's while making preparations for Easter dinner, when out of the blue I started to cry and out of nowhere I heard Spirit say, "You need to go, it is time, it is time to let go." My Spirit was calling out, was I going to listen? Later that day I spoke with my husband about the emotion that was stirring within me and I shared with him what Spirit had said to me, without any hesitation he said, "Go to Sedona and take care of you and don't worry about what is happening here, I will take care of everything." So with John's blessings I called a member of Sunny's team the next day to let her know that I was able to come if there was still an opening, and wouldn't you know the universe was holding a space for me; and before I knew it I was on a plane heading to Sedona. Such awareness came out of this retreat. The following is from an excerpt from my journal:

This morning I realized that I needed to forgive myself for the loss of my innocence, the power and trust that was taken away from me as a child, even though this was the life and the experiences I had chosen when I came into this physical body. The other realization is that I needed to forgive myself for making that choice, the choice that I was not worthy of anything but this, for that I truly forgive myself. I do not regret, for my experiences have been invaluable. In my next life I choose an easier life with the memories of all my past lives.

 TEACHABLE MOMENT: It's all about releasing what was no longer serving me and forgiveness.

I Am Enough

Once my belief systems started to change, I was able to finally tear down some of the walls that my fear built. My spiritual awakening is leading me down the path of self-rediscovery; rediscovering that I am enough. I am becoming more comfortable with my true authentic self as well as my own innate gifts. I no longer have that overwhelming desire to hide behind the many masks of Jenn. I am learning to protect my own energy, maintain boundaries, and release all that is no longer serving me. I have witnessed myself moving toward love with more grace and ease, because I am not getting caught up in my stories. I truly believe when faced with winds for change we find our true direction. I am being called to be of service to others—the healer of oneness—so they too may rediscover their true selves as well as the innate gifts they too behold. What are you being called to do?

Thanks to my husband John for sharing this amazing journey with me and allowing me the freedom to rediscover who I really am. Thank you to Lisa Hardwick for seeing value in my words and creating this amazing opportunity to share my journey as I move toward love. Special thanks to Sunny Dawn Johnston and her entire team for teaching me that I am enough. It is said that people come into our lives for a reason, a season, or a lifetime. I am grateful for each and every person and experience that continues to inspire me every day.

My chapter is dedicated to each of you who have been guided to read this book. May you find comfort in knowing that you are not alone in your journey. Sometimes faced with the winds of change we find our true direction.

~ Jennifer Hamende

Christina Bishop

CHRISTINA BISHOP is a devoted mother of three teenage daughters, a hair designer and makeup artist for over twenty years. Often called a salon psychologist, Christina focuses on love and positive energy to heal any of life's trials. After the death of her husband in 2010, she dove into spirituality. A reiki master, spiritual adviser, life coach, ordained minister, and author. Now unleashing her psychic gifts, she uses all of her lessons and information to help others.

tina.bishop28@yahoo.com

🌿 From Victim To Victor

March 27th, a day I remember yearly, not always celebrated, however, remembered. Many years I sat feeling sad, depressed and angry. Rewind to March 27, 1972. That was a day everyone rejoiced. For a baby girl arrived, a daughter that was planned even. Do you think when I was born that I said, "One day I'm going to become a victim." Absolutely NOT! I came into this world naked and screaming then was swaddled and held. It didn't matter what I did because I was loved, cared for and appreciated.

When we come into this world, the survival mode is simple as long as we have caretakers. Sleep, eat, diaper change, love. Somewhere along the way, we forget that. Survival is not a nice, extravagant home, a Louis Vuitton bag or a Range Rover. Survival is when someone can persevere through anything and when a person can label them self a victor. Many times one falls into the victim mode due to various events in their lives. The definition of a victim according to Webster's Dictionary, is as follows:

victim: \\'vik-təm

1: a living being sacrificed to a deity or in the performance of a religious rite

2: one that is acted on and usually adversely affected by a force or agent <the schools are victims of the social system>

Synonyms: prey, casualty, offering, oblation

I feel this definition is a bit more harsh than the perception one has of the word. Many times children become "the victim" of parents arguing, child abuse, bullying or continual belittling. In any of these instances, it will change the psyche of that beautiful infant who only needed the essentials to a child that feels sad, scared, confused and insecure.

My parents divorced when I was a year old. At this time, my father was awarded full custody of my two older sisters and me. Eight years later, in 1980, my dad remarried a beautiful woman that had two children, a boy and a girl. At first I loved them all very much, as I was happy to have a completed family. Many days I was called ugly by my new step-mother. My stepsister and brother would go shopping all the time with her. Not so for my sisters and me. My father, blind to the emotional abuse, kept funding "her" bank accounts, redecorating "her" home, and buying "her" extravagant gifts. The days of longing to be with my grandparents became more frequent. On Fridays, they would come pick me up for a weekend of shopping and quality time and then return me home on Sunday. It was then I would hear fighting at night through the closed bedroom door. The next day, my new clothes would be gone and my old ones put back in my closet. The insecurity set in. This lasted two years, until my dad left broke, both in his wallet and in his heart.

In this instance, a child was a victim of a dysfunctional relationship. Was she though? Which brings me to my next point. What if this had not happened? Everything in life is a lesson. Every person placed in your life is there for a reason. It may seem unfair, unjust or wrong, however, in my opinion, those that have been through the most *Hell* in life are the most blessed. According to Winston Churchill, "If you are going through Hell, keep going." It is those people, like my eight year old self, that are destined to be life's best teachers, lightworkers, counselors, and advocates. If at age eight, I gave up and blamed every failure in my life on that marriage, I would not be writing this piece today.

As Vince Lombardi said, "Once you learn to quit, it becomes a habit." A victim cannot see the "big picture" of life, but is consumed by quitting because of a small detail that makes up the "big picture." Rather the "big picture" has so many characters, scenes, and bumps to get there. If we reprogram our brains to realize there's a plan bigger than all of our challenges, a plan that brings in different people and obstacles, and a plan that will help us if we let it, then the victim role will be diminished.

In 1986, I was a freshman in high school. I was the girl who went out with boys for a week, only to be left for one of my friends that was willing to do what I wasn't. This led to being labeled a "prude." For homecoming, I was invited to the dance by a popular football player that all the girls wanted. I was insecure about myself, after the mental abuse inflicted on me by my stepmother. I could not understand why this boy was attracted to me. After the dance, he took me out in the middle of nowhere and raped me, and he never spoke to me again. I cried, but I never let anyone know. Apparently, he did though. The girl that was once called a "prude" was now considered a "slut." I was angry, started partying a lot and had an "I don't give a shit" attitude about myself. Once again, I felt abandoned; first by my mother at age one, then a stepmother at age 8 and now a boy at age 14. In the back of my head, I felt I deserved all the negativity that was thrown my way. From that point on, I chose to date bad boys that I tried to fix because that is what I thought I deserved.

The baby born on March 27th, 1972 that came into the world screaming, "Look at me!" was now screaming on the inside. Once again, people were put in my path as lessons, merely pawns in the true big picture.

Confucius says, "It does not matter how slowly you go, as long as you don't stop." I was moving at a snail's pace in my spirituality. I enjoyed a fast life, fun, and partying; anything that would prevent me from helping myself in a positive way. Like many others, I self medicated through alcohol or drugs to help me forget the issues that I should have been dealing with. My teens and early twenties were full of "fun." I partied and had no cares. Although I did have my share of successes, they all ended in heartache and failure. I chalked the successes up to my strength, charisma and personality. My failures were not my fault, but the fault of those that "wronged me" from age one. I was a victim. Looking back now, I hated feeling that way and was miserable. How many people get in that victim mode? It makes your jaw tighten, your stomach hurt and you feel lost and depressed. We feel this way because it is a lower vibration that we are now used to. Our bodies are spiritually programmed from birth to vibrate at a higher frequency, so why do we choose to lower that vibration and get to a place of total despair, of feeling lost, angry, and alone?

I like to think of life as a clock. At birth, both hands are on the twelve. That is when we are all closest to Spirit. We all begin to move from that point as we begin to move through life. For my own personal journey, however, the little hand kept moving further away from that point. For me, it moved from twelve to two during my youth. That was when I experienced my first set of bumps. Then from my teens to early twenties, the hand moved from two to four. That was my second set of bumps. I was not at all prepared for the third set when the hand moved from four to six. This is when I hit rock bottom.

In 1994, I met a Phoenix firefighter and married him a year later. We had three beautiful daughters together, I had a successful job as a hair designer, and we had a beautiful home, nice cars and all the material possessions that should make people "happy." On the outside, I was able to maintain a happy persona, but on the inside, I was crying to be free. The marriage slowly turned from what I thought was love to infidelity, abuse, heartache and pain. The only happiness in my life was my three daughters. I spoiled them rotten, believing that was how people showed love, for my brain had already been manipulated into believing that in 1980.

In my early thirties, I began partying heavily, once again, with my husband this time. I was hoping that by doing this, we could again connect. This was something short lived, for I stopped after that jaw tightening, stomach ache appeared again, for I knew it was wrong. My husband, however, continued. The next years were filled with rehab, broken promises, and more abuse, which eventually led to the little hand of the clock bottoming out at six. How many people get to this point and end it? They give up because they think they were handed this life and that is it for them. They get stuck there. I bet a lot do.

As I hit rock bottom at the six on the "Clock of Life," I was crying all the time because I was exhausted and feeling like a failure. This is when I had an "AHA" moment. "LOOK UP! STRAIGHT ABOVE THE SIX IS THE TWELVE! THAT'S WHERE WE ARE ALL DESTINED TO BE!" The only way back to the twelve is working our way around the clock and back to the top. We do that through *perseverance*.

per·se·ver·ance: \ˌpər-sə-ˈvir-ən(t)s

: continued effort to do or achieve something despite difficulties, failure, or opposition : the action or condition or an instance of persevering.

I was on a mission to get happy. According to Babe Ruth, "Every strike brings me to the next home run." I was done with the strikes. I was now moving toward that home run, the place that Spirit wants us to be. It's the place where all the emotional crap in our lives is removed, cords are cut, and we learn to love the person that matters the most: OURSELVES.

It was time for me to do just that. I loved myself enough to know my life needed to change. If I was to create a better life for my girls and me, I had to leave. I had no money, but I had desire, which was all I needed to make my plan. By October, 2009, I put my plan into action. My husband had been sober for about eight months, but one night he left, and did not return for three days. Upon returning, I questioned his whereabouts, which enraged him. In front of my oldest daughter, he picked me up and threw me down, breaking four of my ribs. That was it. I was not going to be a victim anymore. I was done.

I moved out. It was a lot of hard work and hard times, but I was determined for the sake of my daughters and myself, to make a positive life change. Within six months, the divorce was underway, and I felt a sense of strength and accomplishment even though we had very little money. Somehow it didn't matter because the girls and I had each other. The little hand on the "Clock of Life" began to move toward the twelve. I no longer felt like a victim. One of my favorite quotes from Thomas Edison is: "Many of life's failures are people that did not realize how close they were to success when they gave up." I was not giving up.

My strength was tested, in the blink of an eye, when tragedy struck. On April 7, 2010, I found my soon to be ex husband hanging in his garage. Our world spiraled out of control. I felt as if I was being held underwater with no way to escape. It was this exact moment that many people would have thrown in the towel. I found my inner strength as I hovered in the eye of a hurricane. Anything in my life prior to this, now seemed minimal. The day we laid my girls' father to rest, I looked down at my daughters sitting next to me in the front row of the church, wiped a tear from my eye and looked up. I saw a glorious light beaming through the stained glassed window. This is when I played my life over and over in my head, and I realized that spirit was with me all along.

During hardships, many of us think, "Why ME? This is so unfair. I can't do this." This thinking, however, is just the opposite of how we should be thinking. Our lives, up until we hit rock bottom, are just scenes in the movie of life. Every person who built us up as well as every person (including ourselves) that threw us down, were there for a purpose. Our soul chooses our body. It needs to teach and learn many lessons, just as all those in our lives have to teach and learn their lessons. Our greatest teachers are not those that have had the easiest lives, they are those who have persevered after hitting the bottom.

After this most horrific event in my life, my spiritual side took over. My search for knowledge manifested, and in doing so, I began finding myself. There have been several detours in my quest to get back to the twelve, the place where there is complete love, acceptance and peace. It has been a little over three years since my husband passed, and I am learning to grow daily. Some days I still grieve, but for the most part, I am letting go. I am learning to forgive. I now forgive myself for self-loathing and staying in a victim mode for so long, but mostly I forgive all the people that created the "bumps" in my life. I find myself feeling grateful for all those people, for without them, I would not have learned my greatest lessons. I am now working on being a VICTOR.

 vic·tor: \ˈvik-tər

: one that defeats an enemy or opponent : winner

Synonyms

beater, conquerer, master, subduer, trimmer, vanquisher, winner

In the game of life, we can sit in self-pity (the victim mode), or rather, move forward with strength and perseverance getting back to the twelve mark on the "Clock of Life." Remember, the only way out is through, that is how we will emerge in the great quest to *MOVE TOWARD LOVE.*

Thanks to my late husband Chris, for blessing me with our three daughters: Brielle, Cierra and Madison, who have gone through hell and back with me. I love you. Thanks to my amazing inner circle of friends for always having my back, you know who you are. Thank you to my mentor Toni Spetts, the amount of time you've taken with me is incredible, you truly are a gift from above. Michael, Laurelle, and Baker at peace place in Sedona, Sunny Dawn Johnston, and lastly Lisa and Nancy, thank you for all your support.

Dedicated to my three beautiful souls Brielle, Cierra, and Madison. I am so blessed you are my light. To my late husband Chris Bishop, a soul who left this earth much too soon. My teacher, my guide and now my guardian from heaven above.

~ Christina Bishop

Dawn Amberley

DAWN AMBERLEY was born and bred an English rose, with an endless passion for helping others overcome their limitations and obstacles. A corporate manager by day, by night her alter ego surfaces by providing compassionate care to seriously ill patients and supporting their caregivers.

Dawn now resides in Phoenix, Arizona where she finds wonder in the sun setting on the desert mountains and inspiration in the starry skies at night. She firmly believes that what you give out to the world you get back—ten-fold, so best make it amazing!

dawnamberley@yahoo.com

The Angel Inside Us

February 2010. Surgery Day.

Something was wrong. Something was very wrong. I watched the surgeon walk toward me across the waiting room and trip over a bag on the floor. I'd been waiting for over four hours and was desperate to see his face appear with the news on Martyn's surgery to remove a pancreatic tumor. Once the two hour mark had passed I had started to feel more comfortable that everything was going to plan, but the surgeon's obviously distracted behavior set off an alarm bell in my head, and my concerns were confirmed when he reached me and touched my arm. I knew it was the comforting touch before the bad news.

The surgeon explained with a sad face that he was unable to remove the tumor as there was some cancer that had spread to the liver. Just a little but enough to change the course of action and that a "Plan B" was needed. It took every ounce of strength I had to stand there and listen to him explain about the palliative surgery he'd performed instead, to bypass the tumor to enable Martyn to eat again and at the same time resolve the jaundice. Also that Martyn would be referred to an Oncologist for an aggressive treatment plan. My mind had to take control over my racing heart. I rubbed my left index finger with my right thumb and fingers as hard as I could as a way of keeping me alert and forcing me to take in what he was saying. This news changed everything.

After what seemed an agonizingly long time, I was allowed to go to the recovery room. The surgeon had assured me he would explain the situation to Martyn, but I wasn't sure if he would be awake enough to understand what had happened. One look at Martyn's face told me he knew exactly. "They didn't take it out," he murmured with the little strength he had. "I know," I nodded. I needed to give him a hug but he had so many tubes and wires attached I could barely find a way to get to him. I managed to locate two fingers and held on tightly. I then felt the true meaning of someone searching your eyes for the truth as he asked me what the surgeon said to me. I didn't have any more information than he had already been told, but as someone who had just been given a death sentence, it was as though he was searching deep inside my soul for some answer I couldn't provide.

Martyn was moved to the Intensive Care Unit (ICU) and we spent the evening trying to get our heads around the news while compiling a list of questions to ask the surgeon on his rounds in the morning. At that meeting our fears were confirmed—the cancer could not be cured, but chemotherapy would keep it at bay, maybe for years. He said the important thing was to keep a positive attitude. Easier said than done! Yesterday there had been hope that the cancer would be removed and the focus would be on recovery. Today the focus was on how to survive.

Our History.

Martyn was my "significant other." The relationship between us spanned more than a decade. We had a tumultuous time, in part due to distance as the majority was spent in separate countries while he still lived in our homeland, England. He moved to the US just 2 years prior to the onset of his illness and things started to calm down for us. We realized the reasons why we had stuck together despite all the odds. Both our families were in England so we relied on telephone calls and emails to keep in touch. Martyn also had 4 children in their teens and twenties that he missed tremendously and cherished the times they could visit him here.

The other part of the turmoil in our relationship was due to the fact that Martyn and I were adept at pushing each other's buttons. Both stubborn and single-minded, we were quick to fight and stand our ground on issues. Many times we had to agree to disagree through gritted teeth as neither would back down. Our early days of throwing items across the room in angry frustration turned into a more grown up "walking away" until we both had time to calm down. Sometimes many hours later but more often recently, all it took was a few minutes and peace would be restored. "I still love you," he'd say, meaning he loved me despite the fact that I annoyed the heck out of him. "I still love you too," I'd reply with the exact same sentiment and a frown on my face. A peck on the lips and a flash of his sparkly blue eyes meeting mine and I would soften.

Amongst some of the great things we both shared was a passion for food. We loved to cook together as well as eat out. It didn't matter if it was a tiny hole-in-the-wall place or a lavish restaurant, we loved them all and our days often revolved around what we would cook or what new restaurant we might try next.

The bond between us was pushed to another level entirely when Martyn was diagnosed with pancreatic cancer just 18 days before his surgery. He had been suffering from indigestion pains and back aches but cancer was the last thing we suspected as the cause. In some ways the single-mindedness we both had would ultimately be a useful trait in coping with this battle.

February and March 2010. Trying to move forward.

Martyn was desperate to get out of the hospital and see the Oncologist to find out the action plan. When your options have been cut to the core you find whatever it takes to hold on to, to give you some hope. The only hope now seemed to be chemotherapy. The initial appointment was almost two weeks after surgery and he was still on a liquid diet while his wounds healed. It was like being in a holding pattern. It would be another three weeks after that when chemotherapy would start so that he could build up some strength. He was encouraged by the Oncologist's words that the chemo would be chipping away at the cancer rather than zapping it in a few sessions, and that he'd be in for a long haul. When you're unsure of your lifespan, words like "long haul" can make a huge difference to your state of mind.

Two weeks after surgery, Martyn was given the go-ahead to eat again. "Listen to your body and take it easy," the surgeon cautioned. We stopped at a local restaurant on the way home where Martyn chose what he hoped to be manageable - half a turkey sandwich. He took one mouthful and a look of pure joy came over his face as he went on to savor every bite. I'd come to yearn to see that look again but, unfortunately, it was very fleeting.

The next couple of weeks were full of hospital visits in preparation for chemotherapy: iron infusions, MRI and PET scans; an appointment with a clinical advisor, and minor surgery to have a port fitted in his chest to allow easy access for the chemo drip tube. Martyn was fatigued almost all of the time, his eating was very limited and he was losing around 5 lbs each week. Even at this early stage he was scarcely doing anything for himself. I was holding down a hectic full time job and trying to meet his needs and it was becoming very hard work.

Five weeks after surgery, finally the first chemotherapy session. This was preceded by anti-nausea and steroid drips and everything seemed to go well. That evening Martyn had a little more energy, apparently from the steroids, and was chirpier than he'd been for some time. I was thrilled that he managed a few smiles and that he got up to put a DVD in the machine. Recently he had rarely moved from the couch. Things were looking up! Something else that was short lived.

Chemotherapy was once a week, every Friday. Martyn was even looking forward to the second session just to have some more steroids, but the effect was not as good on the next visit. He was back to being constantly weary. His appetite was very poor but he made the decision to try and eat something small every two hours, as the nurses had often advised. Another thing easier said than done. Many of his old favorites such as Spaghetti Bolognese often caused him either pain or he would just throw them back up. His diet now consisted of soft fruits, yogurts and baked potatoes, just two or three spoonfuls at a time. Any food I made for myself had to be cooked while he was out of the way as he couldn't stand the smell. I ate alone at the table every day and was unable to even eat a snack while anywhere near him. This was such a far stretch from the food loving couple we were once were. I longed for my partner to enjoy a meal with me again. I reminisced about the time he fed me a spoonful of cheesecake as he was eating some himself. "You HAVE to try this, it's sooooo good!" He had a look of ecstasy on his face. It made me giggle then but I wasn't giggling any more. I was achingly lonely. Food represented emotional pain. Food had become a huge gaping issue for both of us.

April 2010. Every day is a winding road.

Martyn perked up again after the third chemo session, so to capitalize on this we went to a local diner for breakfast where he managed to eat one egg on a piece of toast with some fruit. Tears ran down my cheeks. "What's the matter with you?" He looked at me confused. "I'm just so happy you're eating and you're eating with me," I mumbled. My relief was overwhelming.

I realized he had so much on his mind he was not aware of the impact of his actions on me. Most days when I came home from work, he'd be sitting in the dark just gazing into the distance. Sometimes he hadn't even got out of bed all day. He appeared to be very depressed but when I talked to him about it he said he was just so very tired. I plucked up the courage to tell him his behavior was making me depressed and he was upset I hadn't told him this before. What I didn't tell him was that if he asked me to fetch one more thing for him I might explode due to my own exhaustion. Instead, I called the Oncologist's office for advice and the decision was to up the treatment plan to try and deal with his weariness. The next step would be three different types of chemotherapy on a three week plan; once a week for two weeks and one week off. Martyn was eager to move on to the new plan.

Before every chemotherapy session, a small sample of blood was taken to ensure the levels were acceptable to continue with the drugs. I was getting adept at understanding all the acronyms and the consequences of high or low levels of each. At the last session, some extra blood was taken to test Martyn's pancreatic cancer marker levels. This would be the first test since starting chemotherapy and we both had a sleepless night before the nurse's appointment, worrying about what the results would be. At the appointment we were told the marker test hadn't been done! The disappointment was unimaginable. What may have seemed like a simple mistake to them was devastating to a patient waiting for an answer that was critical to his future well-being. I wondered if the nurses, technicians and laboratory staff were really aware of how crucial their actions were and how their words and attitudes could make or break someone's day. How important they had become. How fragile we had become.

Cycle 1 week 1 of the more aggressive chemotherapy schedule went well, but by the second week Martyn's red blood cell count was down. On the way home from that session, I got a call that we needed to go to a different hospital to get blood taken for a match for a transfusion the next day. Somehow I was able to manage work while doing all this driving around. Each hospital was a 60 - 80 mile round trip in various directions. I ran conference calls from parking lots and hospital corridors to try and keep up. My laptop was never far from my side and I worked on emails whenever and wherever I could, such as sitting next to Martyn while he had his transfusion. A couple of days later I got another call that the latest blood work now showed low sodium levels so he had to go in for extra fluids that day, plus even more blood taken for testing. Before this experience when I heard that someone had cancer, I thought it involved just a few trips to the hospital for chemotherapy and some doctors' visits. I really had no idea of the constant running around for treatment and the emotional roller coaster ride that went with it.

While Martyn and I were getting closer by the day and spent quiet evenings together on the couch holding hands, I was becoming more and more estranged from the outside world that wasn't related to cancer. I was in a cancer bubble. I was struggling with the demands of caregiving and although my family and friends were fantastic at supporting me, I really needed to talk to someone who understood my situation. I signed up with an online chat group of caregivers to cancers of all types. Martyn was very against me doing this, convinced that it would be full of needy people who would bring me down, but I was desperate for help so I continued on regardless, and what a Godsend it proved to be. I finally had a safe place to talk about my everyday concerns and even vent some frustrations. I so looked forward to the weekly chats as a way to keep my sanity.

Matters reached a breaking point however when I suggested to Martyn that friends keep an eye on him while I spent time with some visiting relatives who would be arriving in May. He flatly refused saying he would be perfectly okay on his own. The cracks of my exhaustion were starting to show. I had what can only be described as a meltdown. My calm exterior was taken over by a sobbing wreck. I held on to the door frame for strength while I spluttered out how selfish he was and that I was only thinking of him and wanted the best for him. I shook with pent up frustration and anger and barely stopped myself screaming. I left him to his own devices for a few hours, to calm down. When I returned we looked at one another and I fell down beside him while we cried together. Cancer was the pits.

May 2010. The roller coaster derails.

Cycle 2 week 1 went without incident. In fact, the next day Martyn felt so well we planned to go out for a meal. This was our first dinner out since his surgery and so a major event. We felt like a normal couple for once. We shared a meal and he really enjoyed it although he could only eat a small amount. We were both ecstatic at this huge step forward and really felt as though this more aggressive chemo plan was making a big difference. Our joy didn't last long. The next day Martyn was back to being exhausted. By Monday he sat very quietly while I joined the online caregiver chat in the evening. He mentioned his vision was a bit blurry and I checked on the "potential chemotherapy side effects" fridge magnet we had been given at the Oncologist's office. It listed the side effects and when a doctor should be called or when to just monitor the situation. I referenced it frequently. On this check I saw nothing about blurred vision so he just continued resting. Within moments I heard a groan and saw he was having a full blown seizure. I ran between him and typing in the chat room telling them what was going on and asking for advice. "Call 911!" streamed back the replies.

Martyn came around quite fast and quickly re-assumed his stubborn streak. "I'm not going to hospital, I'm fine," he announced. "Put the phone down." After arguing for a while he finally agreed with me taking him to the E.R. When he got up however, he passed out and fell hard on the wooden floor. With that I screamed at him not to move and called an ambulance. He complied. He was taken to the E.R. where his blood pressure dipped to dangerously low levels. I noticed he was not responsive and suddenly a nurse rushed in and tipped the whole bed so that Martyn's head was way below the level of his feet, and immediately attached two bags of fluids to his drip. He came around quickly again, unaware of the drama. "That little incident makes you a candidate for ICU," the nurse sighed. "We'll get you into a room as soon as possible." Our eyes locked, unsure where this new road was taking us.

The next few days were mentally painful. Multiple doctors visited with varying degrees of compassion and opinions. Because each doctor needed his own set of notes, the same questions were asked over and over again. Martyn had to repeat details about his disease multiple times. Sometimes I jumped in with the answers to spare his agony. Pancreatic cancer, yes. Spread to the liver. Stage 4. Unsuccessful Whipple surgery. Palliative surgery performed. Dates, information on the chemotherapy treatment plan and other details were repeated numerous times. I couldn't understand, with modern technology, why all this information had to be restated so often. It was very upsetting to Martyn. As if having terminal cancer wasn't bad enough, it was as though he had to be reminded of it frequently just in case he had forgotten for a moment. Then came the new opinions; that maybe there was more than one cancer, or that it had traveled to his brain, which was why he had a seizure. He was wheeled off for more scans and by this stage was in a state of despair. Thank goodness the scans for cancer in the brain came back negative. There was no spread of it to any other organs. In fact his pancreatic cancer marker levels had gone down. Martyn was relieved beyond words. After a barrage of blood transfusions and liquids he was discharged from the ICU a week later.

My previous concern about Martyn needing care while I had relatives visit during this time had turned out to be a moot point, because he was in hospital during their entire visit.

We returned home different people and were both very scared after the recent events. Martyn had lost a lot of confidence and was unsteady on his feet. I was frightened to leave him alone for more than a few minutes. He wanted me to hold his hand or walk beside him wherever he went. I was more than happy to oblige. All I wanted to do was wrap this man in a healing blanket of love and tell him everything was going to be okay. I wished so much this would be true but this big, brave and strong man was looking pale, drawn, and thin. The cancer bubble was closing in.

June 2010. Together we can do anything.

I tried to remain positive at all costs. Others told me afterwards that they had thought I was being unrealistic, but when you are in a dire situation you only have hope and anything that encourages that hope is a good thing. It's not denial. I had read a book a couple of years earlier called *My Stroke of Insight*, by Jill Bolte Taylor, Ph.D. That book had a profound effect on me and I found myself referring to the words as inspiration on a daily basis. Jill explained how one's energy can have a huge impact on a sick person. How people healing need time, space, quiet and patience. As best as I could I kept my energy around Martyn calm and peaceful. I talked to him in a kind and caring manner. I made eye contact with him and tried to keep a smile on my face. I brushed my fingers over his forehead and rested my hands on his arms or hugged him gently. Just a few months prior, this would have been overly fussy behavior to him but life was very different now. I knew he felt safe in my care and that was the only thing that mattered to me. My whole reason for being was to take care of him. I felt I'd never had a job as important as this. He literally trusted me with this life and how great an honor can you get than that? He thanked me every single day for looking after him and my heart would burst with love for this man. Why did we waste so many years fighting? Why didn't we show this kind of love before now? So many other things took precedence before.

Now we battled everything as one. "Together, we can do anything," he told me.

The Oncologist wanted to continue with the same aggressive chemotherapy plan but reduced by 25%. We went with trepidation but the day passed without incident. Three days later Martyn suddenly passed out again. No seizure this time, but I immediately dialed 911. He actually argued with me while I was talking on the phone but this time I wasn't taking any chances. When the paramedics arrived he argued with them, too! He initially refused to go to the hospital but when they showed him his low blood pressure figures he reluctantly agreed. Back to the ICU. I felt so bad for him. Here was a man used to being in control of everything and now his life was totally out of control and there was nothing he could do about it. "My body seems like it's against me," he would say.

Another week in hospital took its toll on Martyn physically and mentally. He was now starting to gain weight, after he had been constantly losing it every week since the start of his illness. I could see he was gaining fluid. He was still struggling with food and would go all day without eating if he could. He promised me he would try to drink liquid nutrition. He was weak and the exhaustion was all consuming. He was barely able to make it up the stairs, so a bed was moved downstairs for him. Every night I left a telephone by his side and he would use the 'pager' function to call me if he needed anything. I'd hear the ring two or three times a night and run to see to him. One night he didn't page me and at 4:00 a.m. I awoke with a start and rushed to his room only to find he had slept the whole time and was fine; I wasn't sure which of the two situations was more stressful. On the rare occasions he felt well, we would hug in relief that maybe the worst was over only to be dismayed once again within a few hours.

By this time I felt unable and unwilling to leave him at all. He didn't want anyone else looking after him and neither did I. Luckily my job allowed me to work at home and there I stayed. Friends came by with food and ran errands for me. I found it difficult to ask for help but was very grateful when they called to ask if I needed anything while they were already in a grocery store, since I felt I was being less of a burden that way.

I spoke with my family back in England on a daily basis and they provided me with words of encouragement and love. Martyn's children wanted to come over and visit as they did just after his surgery, but he was adamant they shouldn't see him this way. It broke his heart that he couldn't be the Dad he wanted to be. He was getting weaker by the day. His legs became so weak he couldn't walk, and he was still gaining fluids making it difficult to move in bed. Sitting up by himself was almost impossible. We devised a way between us where he would prop himself up on a pillow and then I would bend down and use my shoulder and my body weight to push him to sit upright. We praised ourselves at our ingenuity and our ability to overcome any obstacle together.

We continued to stay optimistic and talked about small accomplishments. Any amount of food eaten was a cause for elation. We tried leg exercises to try and get them working again. The real truth was that a huge black cloud was hanging over us. I was distraught at watching this man waste away before my eyes. I was worn out from keeping up my work life and the demands of caregiving, as well as the pure mental distress that came with it all. Any moment I spent on my own, I spent crying. As Martyn was sleeping much of the time and was unable to move from the bed without my help, I was able to hide this for the most part. I would take a deep breath before I went through the door to see him and retrieved my smile and caring voice. Sometimes I failed and I would berate myself for allowing this brave man to see my tears. "You're such a strong person, I don't understand why you're crying," he would say. I didn't want to let him see my fears. If I couldn't provide him hope, then what was there left? I had to be strong. Inside, I felt as though I was dying with him, little by little. I was scared, every hour, every minute, every second of each day. Ever since his seizure my body was on high alert for any strange sound or any unusual behavior that might signal another disaster. Every time I went in to see him I didn't know what I might find. Sometimes it took all my courage to even go through the door.

Martyn agreed with my request to call Hospice in to give me some assistance. "Anything to make it better for you," he said. "I won't ever forget how upset you were when I refused help." I was shocked at this confession and then alarmed that he had obviously been worrying about it since the day of my meltdown. I would re-live his words repeatedly for many months to come.

By now there was nothing that Martyn could do for himself. I was dedicated to providing 24x7 care and it pushed me past boundaries I never dreamed I would be capable of achieving. "You're an angel," he'd say at least once daily. "In fact, you'd put an angel to shame, with all the things you do for me." I was humbled beyond words. I was grateful the angel inside of me seemed able to cope with anything thrown at her. I wondered where she had come from and how I was able to manage, as life had become very nearly unmanageable.

It almost seemed too much work to bring in Hospice care as there were evaluations and assessments to be done along with a lot of questions and paperwork. This was a great deal for us both to handle. It was a huge relief though that I finally had some real nursing support and a telephone number to call where someone would respond with an actual visit. Among the paraphernalia provided by Hospice was a booklet on "End of Life." This became my new best friend. I read it cover to cover again and again. It gave guidance on signs to look for months, weeks and days before death. I would anxiously look for any signs.

The day of Martyn's birthday arrived but it was no cause for celebration. He was totally confined to bed and could barely keep any food down. He had no interest in opening his birthday cards but did agree to my pleas to call his family back in England. He knew he sounded weak and was scared about upsetting them if they heard it in his voice. He was glad he called, but it exhausted him and he fell straight back to sleep afterwards.

July 2010. Love is all that matters.

Martyn didn't want to talk about death and dying, or even matters of estate or after care. He desperately wanted to get on a plane and fly back to England to live out his days in his homeland, but knew that was not an option. We reduced our expectations and focused on small goals. We celebrated the two small mouthfuls of white rice I spoon-fed him, which he managed to keep down. The irony did not escape me. How life had changed. How priorities had changed.

Work became very frustrating for me when someone would complain about a mistake on a report, or whine about a colleague or some other minor thing. I wanted to scream at them "Try battling with cancer and fighting for your life on a daily basis and see how important that bloody report is then!" I didn't of course. I just kept up the façade and kept on going.

Even if he was sleeping, Martyn liked to know I was close so I would sit on the floor next to the bed with my laptop and grumble away about work problems. When he was awake he would commiserate with me. It made him feel as though he was still part of the human race.

On Friday night Martyn was very uncomfortable and threw up the little amount of liquid nutrition he had managed to drink. He had been prescribed a low dose of morphine, originally to help with increasing his appetite but now also to help with anxiety and sleep. Badly needing to rest, he took a morphine tablet but it made him feel woozy. He appeared to be very restless and confused. I was up almost every hour with him throughout the night. He told me he was not in pain, just didn't feel good. By the early hours I stayed with him on the bed, hoping my presence would at least make him feel calmer. I felt helpless. He made me promise I would not take him to the hospital, but agreed to me calling in the Hospice nurse.

At last Martyn finally settled down. I was so grateful to see him resting and he seemed to be doing better. The nurse hadn't yet arrived, but the Hospice Pharmacy had delivered liquid morphine and anti-anxiety drugs with a syringe and I received instructions over the phone on how to use them. I was terrified. I didn't want to do this. I grimaced and took a huge deep breath as I measured the precise amount of morphine into the syringe and went to administer the dose. What I'd thought was Martyn resting was more like the start of a coma. He was now not speaking coherently. I explained that I was about to put the liquid under his tongue and he was agitated but allowed me to continue. I sat with him and stroked his hair. This appeared to calm him but I just felt sick. Life was spiraling out of control.

The Hospice nurse finally arrived and took Martyn's blood pressure. She took me out to the kitchen to tell me the words I didn't want to hear. "I'm so sorry but he is unlikely to last the night," she announced. How could this be? I was talking to him this morning. Yesterday he got angry about something the nurse said. He still had a lot of fight in him, surely. I'd heard people talk about "taking a turn for the worse" and I guessed this is what they meant. Once the nurse left I immediately returned to Martyn's side and that's where I stayed for the next 14 hours. I squeezed his hand and asked for him to squeeze back if he could hear me, but now there was no response.

I called his children in England and had the daunting task of having to explain this devastating downturn. I held the phone to Martyn's ear while one by one they cried their goodbyes to their Dad. This was utterly gut-wrenching. I tried to find some gratitude inside myself that I was able to provide this service to his children who had no chance to be with him.

My two closest girl friends came to look after me and provided drinks, food and a watchful eye so I could sit and hold Martyn's hand. They took care of everything without me uttering a word. They said the house had an air of love and peace filling it rather than the tension that it had held over the recent few weeks.

Then someone Heaven sent knocked at my door. It was Darren, Martyn's best friend from England, who had been travelling in the US. We knew he was hoping to visit this weekend, but he was supposed to be here to give me a rest and provide a smile for Martyn. Instead Darren was faced with a different prospect. Without a blink he camped out with me in Martyn's room. We reminisced about good times and told stories we thought would make Martyn laugh, chatting as though he was still awake. I thought if it has to end this way, this is how Martyn would want it; the two people he most trusted by his side.

As the hours went by, Darren and I sat quietly talking soothingly to Martyn. Darren had recently lost his father to cancer and so having to witness this again must have been very upsetting, but he unselfishly used his experience to help me understand the dying process and be a solid rock of support for me. When I had time on my own with Martyn, I told him, "It's okay to go, I'll take care of everything. Don't worry about a thing." I looked into his eyes which were still a magnificent blue. I couldn't understand how his eyes were so bright when his body was failing him. It pained me to look at them. When the end drew close I crawled onto the bed beside him and whispered, "I love you." I poured every ounce of love onto him in the hope that it would somehow ease his journey.

Four days after his 52nd birthday, one week after Hospice care started, and five months after the cancer diagnosis, the spirit of Martyn left his body.

Emptiness.

Even though I had mentally prepared for the event, nothing could have prepared me for the reality. My life had been defined by looking after this man and now I wasn't sure what I was put on this earth for anymore. Everything seemed meaningless. I got through each day by putting one foot in front of the other. That was the best I could do. The thought of our love and the sharing of so many precious moments in those last few months carried me through the difficult times to come. I came to realize that Martyn had given me a gift. A priceless gift. He had showed me how to accept love and be willing to give love, unconditionally. Because of that my life was forever changed.

I have written this story to reflect my own personal journey and how these events changed my entire viewpoint on love. I learned that love truly is the only thing that matters. While it cannot provide the answers to all problems, if we approach life with love we cannot fail. I'd also like to think that we all have an angel inside of us who will take over when we need her. With that angel's help we can embrace love and that's how we will survive.

With gratitude to my family and friends who provided endless support—in person, on the telephone and by email. Every thought, every word and every hug was truly appreciated.

Thank you to Martyn for being my best friend. Together we learned that in the end, love is all that matters.

Dedicated to caregivers everywhere who selflessly give their time and support to others. I hope my words shine a light on you.

~ Dawn Amberley

As your mind
becomes clear, so
does your path.

~ SARAH MCCRUM

Zina Bulbuc

ZINA BULBUC is a licensed Heal Your Life® Workshop Facilitator and Life Coach. She is also a published author and holds a Master in Chemical Engineering and an MBA. In 2004 she was the first one to translate and publish Louise Hay's book *You Can Heal Your Life* in Romania. She is curious about life and about the human spirit, and loves to help others by sharing her experiences and knowledge.

She lives in Washington DC Metro area and enjoys the outdoors, travelling, reading, writing and spending time with her friends.

Zina46@gmail.com

Don't Let Fear Be Your Driver

 You are already that which you long to be.

~ JERU KABBAL

There are two major emotions that govern all our actions and decisions: fear and love.

Throughout the history of humankind, we have always longed for love ... And yet, how can we explain that we are the only species on Earth whose individuals use fear for entertainment? How can we explain the fact that violence and crime are the preferred news to watch and they sell much better than any good news? Why are we so attracted to fear? I guess, this is our paradox and we are still trying to figure it out.

Spiritual teachings tell us that our words become our actions and define our lives. I do believe this is true, and based on that I was tempted to write here only about love, so that all I said was positive. But, at the same time I am thinking of all those who live in fear or have a lot of fears they have to confront every day. Talking to them only about love would be as if talking to a hungry child about tasty food, but not telling him how or where to get it. So, I decided to break the rule of positive talk and get into the subject of fear. What is fear? Where does it come from? What does it do to us? How do we deal with it? Most importantly, how do we make the transition from fear to Love. (I purposely used lower case for fear and upper case for Love, for obvious reasons: I wanted to take the power away from fear and acknowledge the magnificence of Love).

The Reality Of Fear

Let's start with the beginning. When does the fear come into our lives? Is a newborn afraid of anything? Or earlier yet, in its mother's womb, is an unborn baby afraid? Let's think about it. We all felt very comfortable before coming out into the world. We were protected, fed, and we didn't have to do anything to 'earn' the care given to us. We were completely trusting of our mother's body to take care of us, and had no fear of anything. It was the same in the first months of our lives: we trusted the adults around us to take care of everything, and all we did was express every need or emotion in a very bold and up-front way. So, from where did the fear come? We learned it. We were taught fear as we grew up. Children all over the world, in all cultures, all religions, all races, are taught fear as they grow up. But why? Why do we need to teach our children fear? Fear of what, or of whom? The more we ask ourselves these questions, the more absurd the answers become. As children, we learn to be afraid of things that not only didn't happen to us, but they never happened to anybody in our family or to any of our friends. Still, some of the fear we learn has to be there to protect us from bad happenings. Some of it though, is useless fear; we drag it along our way through life, we hold on to it as adults, and we are not even aware it is still there. Our task when we grow up is to be able to differentiate one kind of fear from the other.

 It may be hard to hear, but the story of your life is primarily a story of dealing with fears. These aren't the fears of today. They are fears of the subconscious, programmed by the mind-set of a four-year-old. A happy ending can be written only by discovering yourself as you truly are in the present.

~ JERU KABBAL

But what is fear? *Cambridge Dictionary* defines fear as " a strong emotion caused by great worry about something dangerous, painful, or unknown that is happening or might happen."

Following this definition, we could say that being afraid of something that is already happening will get you out of that bad experience. This is the 'good' fear. Being constantly afraid of something that might happen on the other hand may be bad for you. It may stop you from doing things you want or love to do, and in the long run, it may shift the course of your life in the wrong direction. And by 'wrong direction' I mean you don't follow your talents, or dreams or calling. Let's say for instance that you are in an abusive relationship and you live in fear. This fear is there to protect you. This fear is there to tell you to get out. Now, let's say that you would love to dance for living, but your parents sent you to school and you became a successful accountant. Every night you go to bed thinking about your true passion: dancing. But you are afraid to give up a secure and good job, for a dream. You are afraid, because nobody guarantees you that you will be successful as a dancer. This fear is holding you from pursuing your dream; this fear changes the course of your life in a direction you don't really want to go (you just believe that you have to).

Recognize Fear

Another paradox of our society is that on one hand it promotes fear (news, drug advertising, job insecurity, selling insurance for everything you can and cannot imagine), but on the other hand teaches us to hide fears and put on a mask of bravery and success. This is a slippery slope, because many people don't even realize that they live in fear.

Fear of the future is something we learn as children and we continue learning it for the rest of our lives. Remember the little four-year-old that Jeru Kabbal mentioned? Very few people are not afraid of the future. Fear of future is fear of the unknown, fear of darkness. If you could detach yourself from any thoughts for a moment—this present moment—you would feel no fear. Stop reading and just pay attention to this moment. You are sitting or lying down, reading this book. Look at your surroundings, look out the window. There is nothing to fear in this very moment. *Fear of the future is not real.* Anything could change at any given moment between now and the time you placed your fear of the future. And that could make your fear obsolete. Do you create fear by worrying about things that didn't happen? Take a moment and think about it.

Another source of fear of the future is lack of a clear intention in every action. When you are not aware of your intentions, you may create fear. When you act on an automatic pilot, or try to please others, you don't set a clear intention. When you don't set a clear intention, you don't have a clear direction in which to go. You are going into darkness and that creates fear.

Fear of the past on the other hand, is basically a memory of fears you had in the past. Fear of the past disguises itself in beliefs and emotions created by past experiences. *Fear of the past is not real.* Everything that happened in the past is done, finished and gone. It has no power on you and your actions today, unless you choose so. Are you afraid of things from the past? Did you grow up in a fear-based system - a country governed by dictatorship, or a family with an abusive parent? Did you experience a frightening event or an accident in the past that still haunts you? How does holding on to those memories of fear influence your actions today?

Fear of being judged, fear of not being good enough, fear of being shamed or rejected, are all an expression of the ultimate fear. These kinds of fear are more common than we think and they are often hidden behind the need for perfection. Next time you will meet people that describe themselves as being perfectionists, you will see more about them than it meets the eye. If you are that person (I was), it is time to look a little deeper for the reason why you are a perfectionist. There is no negative connotation to being perfectionist; on the contrary. But, if there is fear behind it, it is a good idea to identify that fear, look it in the eyes and deal with it.

Fear is feeling powerless. That generates anger, depression, and resentment. You can recognize fear in all negative emotions you are feeling. Next time you feel angry or frustrated, stop for a moment and try to find out what is behind that anger or frustration. Ask yourself "why am I angry?" Then, whatever the answer is, ask yourself again "why is this?" and then again, "why?" for the next answer. After answering a few times to "why?", you will find out that is the fear that caused it in the first place: fear of losing power, fear of not being heard, or not being appreciated, fear of not being loved, fear of not belonging, fear, fear, fear...

When you feel powerless, you look outside for help and if it didn't come in the form you expected, you are disappointed and that makes you more depressed and increases the fear.

When you look outside for help, you may believe that if one problem or another would be solved in your life, you wouldn't be afraid anymore.

This is just an excuse and you are hiding behind it. You will certainly find something else to worry about and create a new fear. Let's say for instance you are afraid of not having a sufficient income after you retire. You may believe that if you won the lottery, all your fear would be gone. But, after winning the lottery, you will discover that while you don't worry about money anymore, you are afraid of getting sick and not being able to enjoy your money. Why? It is because your fear originates in your lack of trust in yourself, not in the lack of money. You don't need to look outside for help, in order to heal your fears. Fear is always where there is no trust. *If you trust yourself truly and completely, you cannot be afraid.* The reverse is also true: conquering your fears helps you build trust in yourself.

Fear may have come into your life to guide you to trust yourself.

How To Deal With It

Are you afraid? Think of the fear as an entity that lives on your expense. You have to feed it every day (and mostly every night before you fall asleep), with fearful thoughts. *Let your fear starve.* How? Just change your thoughts. Replace any fearful thought with the opposite positive thought and set your clear intention for what you *want* to have, to achieve or to feel. Ask yourself what makes you hold on to your fear? What do you resist? Do you use fear to avoid something? What is it you want to avoid? Be as honest as you can when answering these questions, and you may find your way out of fear. Think of all fearful things that happened to you as gifts. What if they came into your life to give you the chance to overcome them and prove to yourself what you are made of? Or better said, to discover your own magnificence.

Don't allow fear to drive your bus: use it as a tool for self-discovery; use it as a tool to build self-esteem.

Living fearless means to trust yourself, and trusting yourself means you let go of all your mind-created limitations. We set our own (unjustified) limitations, not from what we feel in our heart we *can be* or we *can do*, but from what others tell us what we *should* be and do. This is how we learn fear. It has been proven many times in our history as human species, that we are much more than we believe we are. And every now and then, somebody would stand out from the crowd to remind us of our magnificence, of our divinity. Living fearless means you recognized your own divinity and you live in harmony with yourself, with your soul. *If you fully trusted yourself, you couldn't be afraid of anything.* Imagine how that would feel; imagine what kind of life would you have. Spend one more moment to feel and see yourself living that fearless life ...

The Path To Love

We already know that where there is love, there cannot be fear. Let's have a closer look at how the two are related (or not).

Let's take the example of fear of being judged. I would estimate that more than ninety percent of people are afraid of being judged. Where is this fear coming from? We talked earlier about learning fear as children. This is probably one of the first fears we learn. What is behind this fear of being judged? To answer that, we will need to have a look at us as a society governed by rules. Since ancient times, we continuously created rules. We evolved, and our rules evolved as well. They became tougher and tougher, stricter and stricter, until we reached a point where it is very hard for us to keep up with our own rules. And when I say rules, I don't mean legislation; I mean un-spoken and un-written rules that set the values of our society. For instance, consider how being successful is defined. You have to be famous, and have a lot of money and have some kind of top job. Ninety percent of us are not famous, and don't have millions of dollars. Does it make us un-successful? Of course not! But the unspoken rules make us believe so. So how do we get out of this thinking pattern and let go of the fear of being judged (or better said, 'misjudged'). The fear of being judged has its roots in a lack of self-trust. I asked you earlier to imagine how your life would be if you lived a fearless life. Now try for a moment to imagine how would your life be if nobody around you would have any criticism at all for you. How would you act if everybody would completely approve and support you at all times? It is hard to imagine, right? I had difficulties imagining that too. If that would be true, then this would be how real Love feels. Let me go back to our previous thought: *you cannot be afraid of being judged if you trusted yourself.* Trusting yourself is easy when you are living in a loving environment. Although it shouldn't be like that, it is still true that trusting yourself when you don't live surrounded by love is extraordinary. It shows a strong connection with your essence, it shows you recognize and know who you really are. And this is exactly the point. Love comes from within, not from outside. If you trusted yourself (which is the same as loving yourself) enough to act as if there was no external criticism, people around you would start to respond with love. Or, those who criticize you would slowly distance themselves from you, and you will make new friends who respond to your love-sourced actions with love.

If all of us could act from love and attract love reactions from everybody else, this world would be pure joy. It is interesting though, how our most terrifying emotion is joy. We are afraid of experiencing joy. We learned fear, so we are now afraid of too many good things in our life, because something bad will happen, to counteract the joy. Did you notice that when we are overwhelmed with joy we cry? I always wondered why couldn't we express intense joy in a different way? Crying is for sad occasions, crying is for when we hurt.

Our natural state is meant to be joy. We just judged ourselves out of joy and magnificence, and we started to be afraid.

So how do we go back to Joy and Love? In small and simple steps: if you are afraid that you have no support and nobody would help you, go out and help somebody who needs it; if you are afraid that people don't like you, try every day to compliment three people you meet. It is that simple. The more love you give, the more love comes back to you. Love never runs out.

And even if sometimes we need a little practice to get back to being familiar with Love, it is worth the effort.

Recognize Love

There are a lot of people, who against all odds, had the strength to act from a place of love; there are many that still do. They are our heroes, our teachers and our masters. They trusted themselves enough to act as if nobody ever criticized them, even though sometimes the external criticism was beyond endurance. They proved to us that we are all magnificent beings, we are divine and we are coming from a place of Love. Mahatma Gandhi, Jesus Christ, Martin Luther King Jr., Nelson Mandela, Mother Theresa, Dalai lama, are just a few that showed us what the human spirit is made of. With gentleness and love, they changed this world forever. Were they afraid? I will let you answer this question...

 Our deepest fear is that we are powerful beyond imagination.

~ MARIANNE WILLIAMSON

So, what is Love? *Cambridge Dictionary* defines it as: "to have a strong affection for someone, which can be combined with a strong romantic attraction." Did you smile? Me too. Yes, it is sad, but true: when talking about fear, all is well known and covered; but when we talk about love, dictionaries didn't catch up with all aspects of love, didn't catch up with our spiritual evolution. What this definition of love talks about, is rather lust. True love, Love with a capital L, is unconditional, compassionate and wonderful. Many of us are not prepared to receive this kind of Love, and if we get a glimpse at it, we either feel overwhelmed, or we cannot find words to describe it. That explains why we teach our children fear and not Love. We know more about, and are more familiar with fear.

So, how can we all act from a place of Love? To act from a place of (inner) Love, means you trust yourself, means you love yourself.

You know you love yourself enough when you don't feel you betray yourself through your actions.

You know you love yourself enough when you can compromise without feeling that you were robbed. On the contrary, compromising will make you feel generous.

You know you love yourself enough when you are at peace with your decisions.

You know you love yourself enough when you are forgiving with others.

You know *you love yourself enough when you are not afraid.*

Living in fear is darkness. Living in Love is Light. We all can make the transition to Light.

 A miracle is a shift in perception from fear to love.

~ MARIANNE WILLIAMSON

I wish you Love.

To my cousins and friends who stood by me for the past two years, thank you!

Ane, Aura, Cristi, Doina, Francoise, Gabriela, Maryann, your names are forever engraved in my heart.

My dear friend and coach Andrea Walters, you helped me decipher, understand, and conquer my fears. This story is for you.

~ Zina Bulbuc

Tammy Lagoski

TAMMY GYNELL LAGOSKI is a published author, publishing consultant, and is knowledgeable in Grief Coaching and working with diverse populations. She was raised on a farm in Charleston, Illinois and currently resides in Peoria, Illinois, where she enjoys spending time with her husband/best friend and traveling with him to visit their children and grandchildren. She also enjoys spending time with her two dogs, Francie and Molly, who are as rambunctious as a couple of two year olds.

tammylag@gmail.com
www.tammylagoski.com

Threads of Love, Grace, Faith, and Goodness

For several months, I have been pondering on the title of our new book, "*Move Toward Love*," and what I really had to say or contribute on this subject. Countless thoughts meandered through my mind stopping here and there gathering inspiration along the path.

In my quest, I conjured up several concepts that at first glance, did not seem to have any connections or threads weaving them together. As in any piece of artwork made out of fabric, one needs to gather fabric with vivid hues and patterns along with rich threads. When creating a vision of love, my design would use samples of God's love for us, our love for him, our love for others and self-love; thus, a beautiful creation evolves for one to touch, to feel and to hold in our hearts and souls.

The journey into what is God's love can be quite simple or complex ... perhaps a little of both. The Biblical sense of God's love for us is unconditional love regardless of our looks, our attire, our riches, jobs, etc. He loves us despite our arrogance, naivety and stubbornness. God believes in us and encourages us to be our best, but even when we falter in life and our "best" is a mass of failure, he loves us. He is patient with us even when we become totally deaf and perhaps immune to His words. Thankfully, for us God forgives us our worst sins that we may create or act upon.

In life, it isn't always easy for humans to forgive each other let alone self. Thus becomes the next stage of love: love, acceptance and forgiveness of self.

Herein lies my problem, loving and accepting myself for the human being God made me.

For years I have struggled with low self-esteem and in truth, I still struggle today. Looking in the mirror I see this over weight aging lady who has not accomplished anything in her life. Heck, I would love to have hobbies but, I can't sew, can't draw, knit, crochet or any of the things I wish I could do. My projects turn out like a little preschooler's attempt. Cooking, I am mediocre. Well, there are two or three dishes I make pretty well …

Smart, well, sometimes I am and sometimes I am not. Sadly, when I need to be smart my brain seems to have disappeared leaving me open mouthed and looking dumbfounded.

Do you see a pattern emerging? Some of the things I have mentioned are our perceptions of how other folks see us, because that's how we see ourselves. Thus, when we are around someone whom we perceive to be smart, gorgeous, skinny, gifted and the "bomb" we diminish our own self by comparison. The ugly monster is gaining momentum. How can we love others, if all we see is ugliness when we look in the mirror? When you look in the mirror your reflection bounces back the images you see or think you see … not only in yourself, but people you come in contact with on the phone, at work, at home, in the grocery store, etc.

Some might think self-love is selfish because we focus on our body, goals, dreams and affirmations. Discovering where the cliff of selfishness plunges, versus where the passage to loving God, self and others merges is a journey that is not for the faint of heart.

I would like to share something from the Bible as well as a quote from John Stott that I found inspirational and brings love home for me.

"But the fruit of the Spirit is love, joy, peace, patience, kindness, goodness faithfulness, gentleness and self-control. Against such things there is no law."

~ GALATIANS 5:22-23

"... Love issues an action. For if love is the first fruit of the Spirit, with joy and peace following in its wake, the next comes patience, kindness, goodness. Love is not romance, let alone eroticism. It is not even pure sentiment or emotion. It sounds abstract, but it leads to positive attitudes and concrete actions, namely, 'patience', 'kindness', and 'goodness'...

~ JOHN STOTT

Loving God, and learning to love self provides the pivotal road to loving others. Ah, another journey and mountain to climb, loving others. It surprises me how hard it is to love others, especially family. Family. What feeling does this word conjure up; anger, pride, happiness, comfort, fear? Personally, my family evokes many emotions in me. Sometimes it's aggravation, impatience, and frustration. My siblings and I have an interesting relationship. Each one of us is head strong and opinionated. When we have family gatherings the discussions can become quite lively! In fact, there are weeks and months we may not speak to one another due to some perceived misunderstanding. Currently, we are at odds over my father's care. He has Alzheimer's disease and requires 24/7 care. At first, my siblings tried to keep him at home, but fights and arguments ensued about money, and how one sibling or another was treating my father. Meetings with the Senior Citizen Advocate transpired. Court dates; hearings and lawyer appointments wrapped my family in bondage of anger and resentment. Currently, my dad is in the nursing home and one sibling is the Power of Attorney, which elicited anger and more resentment among the family. Some days a couple of the siblings get along, but more often than not, those days are rare. Finding a balance of love and acceptance for family members is not an easy task. As I write this chapter family relationships are split, but despite the anger and dislike one may feel for a sibling, we still love each other. We may not like one another, but there is love. Have you seen siblings and family members come close to blows with one another one minute and ready to attack an individual who has the audacity to put down, or attack their sibling? Well, that's my family. Despite our tempers and strong opinions we are bonded by our mutual love.

Lastly, we are faced with love of strangers. As human beings we are taught to love and be kind to our neighbors, but sadly, this is not how it plays out in real life. While watching the news and reading the headlines in the newspaper it became apparent that we are not a tolerant and loving nation. Despite folks declaring to be open minded and accepting of others values, we have become intolerant of folks who do not believe in the same religion, morals, social issues or political beliefs. I urge you to take a look at comments people have made after reading an article on politics, religion, gay rights, Christianity and comments made on Twitter and Face Book. The cruelty of these comments is horrendous. Personally, I am shocked at the comments I've read. On occasion, I have even written a response to an individual regarding their cruel words. I hesitate in using the term chastise, but I guess that is exactly what I have done. Sadly, I am wasting my breath as the author of the original comment usually comes back with their swords blazing at my words and the fact that I had the audacity to chastise them for sharing their worldly views.

In recent months, the news headlines have been focused on trials dealing with murder and social issues which caused me to think about the "what if's" … What if a young man went straight home instead of turning back to confront the stranger following him. What if a young adult stayed in his car and waited for the police, instead of getting out of his car and confronting the young man? Would that young man be alive today? Perhaps, the events may have ended positively and not in death. Sadly, the outcome of each man's actions caused riots, anger and hate to explode across the nation and world. In this day and age, you would think progress really has been made and acceptance of different races would not be an issue, but blacks and whites are at more odds now than in the past. Currently, bickering has become an issue, as the Gay community condemns Christians and Christians rebuke the Gay community; in addition, there are more cultures and religions fighting for freedom against oppression, and terrorists killing Americans in mass quantities. Why do I dare bring up these issues? Because we are living in a time where humans are supposed to be open and tolerant of one another, but alas, that is far from the truth. What happened to loving someone without judging him or her? What do you think God sees when he looks down upon his children? Do you think all the hate and anger makes His heart swell with love and pride? No, I don't think so. My belief is that God wants us to love each other unconditionally. Does that mean we agree or accept a persons beliefs, or lifestyle? No, what it means is this; we can love without being cruel, judgmental and full of hate. If one wants to show God's love, then we must act with love, not hate or anger. Can we disagree, sure! Personally, I have friends of different faiths, religions, and lifestyles. Do I believe in certain rights, or in certain religions, not necessarily? Does that mean, I am going to hate my friends for their lifestyles or beliefs, no. In fact, I love them dearly for the person God created them to be. In the Christian world, folks may think I am dishonoring God by accepting my friends for being Gay, Buddhist, or Muslim, or whatever lifestyle they favor. Sadly, that is far from the truth. I love my God and I truly feel he wants us to find a way to love each other. I believe in the old adage, "you win more folks over with honey than vinegar." An example of vinegar, really venom would be riots, acts of terrorism and murders. Do you think these horrendous acts toward fellow human beings will bring about love, agreement and cohesion? Sadly, these acts breed upon each other and before long; cells start building upon each other creating a mass of hate. What if we could avoid riots, murder and terrorism? What if we humans followed the premise of patience, love, kindness, gentleness and self-control? Maybe, just maybe the world would be a more peaceful loving world. So, you are thinking, "Who are you kidding? Are you a Polly Anna? No I am not naïve and blind. I am just asking, what if …

Speaking of God and Christianity sometimes we Christians turn off folks by our self-righteous acts and behaviors. We proclaim to love God and to obey his tenants. Which is okay, but how far will we go in our beliefs in turning someone away who really needs help, physically and spiritually? This past month or so, a dear friend had a serious situation occur within her family. This lady loves God with all her heart and fully practices her faith. Alas, she found out her homeless brother needed help moving his items from one storage unit to another and a ride to the bus station in order to take the trip to her home where he would have refuge and receive the help he needs. My friend called many churches only to be turned away. None of the churches offered this kind of help or service. Honestly, we were all appalled at the lack of care and stewardship these churches offered. After much prayer, two friends on Face Book came to his rescue. My heart was heavy when I read the post from this lovely friend and lady. Once again, love, patience, kindness and generosity was not fostered; therefore, souls were dashed and hope almost dampened out.

Understandably, this chapter may offend folks because I do talk about my God and faith. I do not expect you to get down on your knees and turn your heart and eyes to my God; since that would be naïve. What I want you to really see is this ... moving toward love requires many acts of love and faith, not anger, spite, malice or rejection. Moving toward love is learning to be forgiving to have faith in each other despite our weaknesses, beliefs or lifestyles. Please stop and recall the words I used earlier:

 "... Love issues an action. For if love is the first fruit of the Spirit, with joy and peace following in its wake, the next comes patience, kindness, goodness ..."

~ JOHN STOTT

Usually when I write, I write about my faith and how it helped me through various trials and tribulations. This time, I chose to focus not only on self, but human kind and the serious issues that prevent us from moving toward love. May you find peace and love in my words and not hate, rejection or a judgmental attitude, but one of grace, love, kindness and goodness.

To Alice Lou Gramann, thank you for mentoring and believing in me. Because of you, I fulfilled my dream of becoming a Librarian.

To Mary Downing, my dear friend and mentor. Mary, thank you for believing in me, guiding me and supporting me throughout the years.

To Karen Egan for encouraging me to "Think Outside the Box."

Lastly, to the Illinois State Librarians, who are dedicated in serving the patrons and libraries under their tutelage. I admire and respect you all ...

Thank you to my grandmother, my mother and aunt, who are akin to Lucy and Ethel, and my daughter, Mara. Toss us together, and we become a mass of laughter and tears. Chuck, thank you for loving me and accepting the quirky lady that I am. I love you more than infinity.

~ Tammy Lagoski

Purpose is what gives life a meaning.

~ CHARLES H. PERKHURST

Shellie Couch

SHELLIE COUCH is an author and creator and owner of Practice Living Joy, where she provides group and individual coaching and workshops on the art of living with joy in the present moment. She is often called upon as a speaker on the topics of the power of joy and overcoming personal obstacles.

She resides in rural Inman, Kansas with her husband. She enjoys spending time with her three adult children and her two grandchildren. When not writing or teaching, she enjoys spending time traveling or reconnecting with nature.

www.PracticeLivingJoy.com
shellie.couch@practicelivingjoy.com

Weave Me The Sunshine

Weave, weave, weave me the sunshine out of
the falling rain. Weave me the hope of a new
tomorrow, fill my cup again.

~ PETER YARROW

Weave me the hope of a new tomorrow. Boy, can I remember a time
when that was all in the world that I desired. The days were so
incredibly bleak. I could not see anything but despair. Things that were
supposed to bring me joy left me flat. A sense of accomplishment was
hard to find, and just making it through another day was the biggest
accomplishment that I could hope for.

How long had this been going on? Days, weeks, months? I don't know
for sure, but long enough that my loving husband was insistent that I
seek help. I wasn't being fair to him, not to our children, not to myself.

Seek help? How could I do that? Didn't he know that asking for help
would be admitting that I wasn't normal? I would be labeled. I would
be "officially" crazy if I sought help.

He had been asking for years. Now he had moved past asking. He was
telling me that I had to do this. I had to go to a doctor. A psychiatrist.
A doctor for crazy people. Didn't he know how hard that was going to

be? To admit that, yes, I have a mental defect. What happens then? Once you have that label? Does it follow you around and make life more difficult? Do you have to explain it away all the time? Does it make it easier? Do you just do whatever you want to do and then blame the diagnosis—"Oh well, I am crazy, so it doesn't matter?" I can just hear people discussing me. "Shellie? Oh, don't mind her. She is crazy. Really. She was diagnosed." I can hear them whispering the word "crazy" like some people do when they speak of cancer.

I did go, though. I went to find the help that I needed. I did need it. I wasn't used to feeling this down for this long. Usually, my life was a roller coaster of emotions. I generally went from feeling wonderful and like I could accomplish anything to being agitated and angry that things weren't working as they had in my head, and finally to being sad and tired and crying. Usually that happened in a fairly regular and quick succession. The span from one extreme to the other was usually four or five days at most, sometimes only two or three days. But this, this sad and tired and lethargic spell, had been going on for quite a while.

The day of my appointment arrived, and I told the doctor only what was necessary to help him to help me out of this depression. I didn't tell him about my usual roller coaster emotions, only that I had an unreasonable feeling of sadness and doom that I hadn't been able to shake. He didn't really press me about historical behavior, and I was careful not to offer him any more than I thought he needed. I didn't think it was necessary to tell him about the loud voices in my head. I didn't need to be labeled with *that kind of crazy*. I rationalized to myself that it wasn't like the voices were telling me to do things. I couldn't even really make out what they were saying, anyway. It was just like a huge group of people talking all at once in a room that echoed. It was just so loud.

The doctor gave me medication. The medication helped. I was feeling much better in just a couple of days. I was feeling really good within a week. Then I made a decision that would forever change my life. The really good feeling was beginning to wear off a bit as I acclimated to the medication. I called and asked for an increased dose of medication. It was approved. I didn't even have to go back in. The doctor's nurse just called it in to the pharmacy and I went to pick it up.

I picked up the new, increased dose of medication and started it right away. I was on a high such as I had never been on in my life. I felt that I could do whatever I wanted to do, that I was entitled to do whatever I wanted to do and that there would be no consequences for any of my choices. I was so sure of myself and my capabilities that I decided I no longer needed medication. I stopped taking it.

I crashed. I crashed hard. With the medication that was helping me maintain the mania no longer in my system, I was plunged into the deepest darkest depression that I had ever known. The sense of remorse for the crazy antics during the mania just added to the sense of doom. I gave up in a big way. I ended up hospitalized, in a locked psychiatric ward.

I tell you all of this because this has been very difficult for me to move toward love of the diagnosis, the label. While I have been able to overcome the symptoms of the diagnosis, and am now medication free, the actual label of "Bipolar Disorder" is something that I have kept hidden and have been ashamed of. I have mentioned it in order to better illustrate my journey to joy from time to time, but, for the most part, it was something that I kept in the closet. Not just in the closet—in a locked box in the bottom of the closet, covered with lots of other stuff—anything to keep it as hidden as possible.

Through the years of finding my way through the symptoms of the illness, I learned many lessons about moving toward love, but learning to accept and even embrace the label and the diagnosis eluded me.

I think that it is in all the learning to combat, overcome and finally manage the symptoms of the disease that I finally, just in the last few months, have come to accept the diagnosis, to move toward it with nothing but love. I have recently found that in embracing that it is a part of me, I am able to move forward into my power.

It has been in all of the lessons that I have been learning over the course of my journey that I can see what has really worked for me. It is what has continued to bring me closer to seeing this aspect of my life with love. It is what is allowing me to come into the person that I am meant to be, the person that I have dreamed of being.

 Well I've seen the steel and the concrete crumble,
Shine on me again. The proud and the mighty all
have stumbled, Shine on me again.

~ PETER YARROW

Steel and concrete crumbling? Proud and mighty stumbling? Yes. That was me. I thought that I was made of steel and concrete, indestructible. I was proud and mighty, and yet with that single episode in my life, I thought that my pillars were crumbling. I really thought that with that diagnosis, that label, I could no longer stand proud and mighty. I felt shame and I felt that I would be judged for that label. Yet, that time of my life is the very one that, today, I am most grateful for.

Appreciation is the most wonderful gift that we can give ourselves. Throughout these years of my journey to joy, learning to appreciate has been one of the things that has made the most difference. I learned to appreciate every experience, good or seemingly bad, and I always look for the positive in every single experience. I learned to do that with the experiences of living with periods of mania and depression, but I had never learned to do that with the experience of receiving a diagnosis, a label. Once I began to talk about having the diagnosis and how I had learned to live with the label, I was truly sharing my truth. It is a part of who I am, although it doesn't define me. Once I was able to speak to that, and empower others to do the same, I began to truly accept it and move toward it with love.

I thought, for the longest time, that the only upside to having Bipolar Disorder was that it brought me into the search for a more joyous life. I was able to learn about myself in a way that I hadn't been open to prior to my hospitalization. I was able to learn management skills that helped me not only cope with the inherent ups and downs, but to thrive with them ... to make them work FOR me instead of against me. I have recently come into the realization, though, that the diagnosis and label that I feared so much have been a huge gift to me. I understand, now, that I was still acting from a place of fear around the labels and stigma that come with a mental health diagnosis.

I hadn't been following my own advice and listening to the universe about the gifts that had been given to me. The universe had been sending me messages, and I had been sending those messages to voicemail, unwilling to hear them. I would speak at a gathering and share my story of finding joy through all the craziness that I had endured in life, through attempting suicide, through being raped, through being hospitalized and diagnosed with Bipolar Disorder—and the thing that always got the most comments, the most positive feedback, even though I would only briefly touch on it, was the fact that people could relate to being diagnosed with a mental illness. They could feel the pain of feeling labeled and feeling 'less than' because of the stigma involved. I would walk away from those speaking engagements feeling frustrated and hurt that the people hadn't heard my message. I felt like my message was a message of finding joy, and all they were hearing was that I had gotten past the label and stigma of mental illness. What I failed to realize and understand was that these people *were* hearing my message. It was I who had failed to hear it! My message was one of finding joy, but it was also one of overcoming the label and stigma of mental illness. I was negating that they had heard exactly what they had needed to hear, and in limiting my focus away from that topic, not only was I detracting from my own authenticity, I was failing to hear the universe tell me that my one desire in life, to help others, was being pushed away by my failure to allow it.

 If only I could heal your sorrow, shine on me again, I'd help you to find your new tomorrow, shine on me again.

~ PETER YARROW

I began to change how I was looking at that area of my speaking and about the comments that were coming from it. I began to hear those comments with love instead of frustration. I began to think that I could heal some sorrows that others had around those areas, but we all know that I can't heal someone else, I can't help them find their tomorrow. What I could do, though, is to continue to apply the lessons that I have learned throughout my journey: looking for and finding the gift in any situation, appreciating the gift and moving toward it with love. I, instead, began to appreciate their stories and to appreciate that I was able to help them feel safe enough to share their stories. I began to look for the gift in the label. I started asking the universe to show me what was right in the label and the stigma. In beginning to learn to move toward love about my diagnosis and the labels and stigmas that surround it, I am learning to empower others to do the same. If others are able to do the same, perhaps, in time, there will not be a stigma surrounding mental illnesses, or if the stigma sticks around, that those with those diagnosis will at least be able to find joy in where they are and see the gift in it, too, and to make it work for them instead of trying to work against it.

 Only you can climb the mountain, shine on me again, if you want a drink from the golden fountain, shine on me again.

~ PETER YARROW

My greatest joy is in knowing that in everything, I continue to grow, to expand and to move toward love. Sometimes, even when you think you have overcome something, have placed it behind you, you can still find room to move toward it with love in a way that was unexpected. But, only YOU can climb the mountain, only you can choose to look at situations through the lenses of love. Think about that experience that has caused growth, the one that you feel like you have conquered. Is there a way to see it with more love? Would it serve you in great and unexpected ways if you were able to do that? What about the experience that you are going through now? The one that you are thinking, "If I can just get past this, everything will be okay?" What would happen if you looked at it as a gift and anticipated the wonderful result of it with lots of love? Would you find that that viewpoint would serve you in great ways? This is my challenge to you today: Look at the challenges and hardships that you have now with love and see them as the gift that they truly are. Move toward it with love.

I would like to thank the amazing and abundant universe for all of the wonders that it has shown me, my fellow authors whose friendship has become invaluable, and my family whose love and support warms my heart and soul.

Dedicated the man of my dreams, who has supported me in so many ways along this journey in life, my husband, Coil.

~ Shellie Couch

A ship is safe in
the harbor, but
that's not what
ships are for.

~ WILLIAM SHEDD

Beryl Huang

BERYL HUANG, Founder of the American Institute of Attitudinal Psychology, is a leading attitudinal psychologist helping thousands of people each year through her private and group sessions in motivation, self-improvement, hypnotherapy and past life regression, as well as seminars and workshops in America and Asia. She has been featured in media in North America and Europe and hosts two TV talk shows on Chinese television and a radio live call-in show in Southern California.

https://www.facebook.com/DrBerylHuang

Don't hate, just love

When China lost the war with Japan in 1895, Taiwan was ceded to Japan as a colony and the Japanese occupied Taiwan from 1895 to 1945.

In 1944, the Japanese captured my grandfather who was a mayor and community leader; they forced him to work for them because my grandfather could speak both Chinese and Japanese fluently. They wanted him to rule other Chinese and put those people who won't obey in jail to torture or kill. My grandfather refused, and as a result they murdered him in front of my grandmother and my then only 3 years old mom and 2 years old uncle. They then put them in jail and threw away my grandfather's dead body like garbage with no proper respect of funeral to the couture (in Taiwanese culture, when someone dies, it is very important to have a proper funeral so that the person can go to heaven). If it wasn't for some kind-hearted people who saved them from jail and helped them escape ... today, there would definitely be no *me* here to share the story with you.

I was not the one who went through such a horrifying experience; I can only imagine how terrified and scared my family was. Do I like what happened? Do I like what the Japanese did to my family? Of course not: who would? The only item I have about my grandfather is an old black and white, almost completely faded picture of him. Nothing else. My grandmother never remarried nor had another man in her life after all, but guess what, till the day she died, she NEVER allowed us to hate, to be angry, to talk about revenge. As a teenager, after I learned history in school about what happened between China, Taiwan and Japan in World War II, I once was so frustrated I asked her, "Why don't you hate Japanese? They killed your husband, they made my mom and uncle have no father when they grew up, why do you still want us to forgive?" I almost yelled at her when I asked her the question so you can imagine how angry I was.

She told me, "Things have already happened. There is no way we could go back to turn history around. Yes, it was such a heartbreaking event, but there is nothing I could do but keep strong and move on with life. I was only grateful that I was able to receive help to assist me and your mom and uncle survive. I am thankful every day when I wake up and every day is better than yesterday. I will never forget what they did to your grandfather and our family, but I choose to forgive them so I can have peace in my heart and go on with my life, and because I forgive, so I was able to pass each day and not give up the life your grandfather sacrificed for us. Don't hold onto anger, hurt or pain. They steal your energy and keep you away from love."

When we look back to the history, there are too many things that happen in the world now which are hard to forgive. Although it is hard to forgive those who have done such acts, if we acknowledge God's forgiveness in our soul for all the small and huge mistakes we have committed, we can forgive even those who hurt us the most. Remembrances of all the sadness in history do not only open our eyes and minds, they also solidify the essence of forgiveness over pride. Yes, the Japanese soldiers did something bad, but that doesn't mean all Japanese are bad people. It was a different time in history and one that we can all learn from.

Just as important, nor should we judge others since we aren't perfect ourselves. Forgiving is not agreeing with the wrong. Forgiving simply means we are releasing ourselves from the chains of not forgiving; we free ourselves from the slavery of bitterness and resentment. Forgive what has hurt us, or things we can't change, but never forget what we have learned from the past.

Are you holding in frustration and anger waiting for an apology? If so, forgive them even if they are not sorry. Instead of holding on to something that is deteriorating your heart and mind, it might be time to move on. Move on, not because there is something better out there than what you are experiencing in the moment, but also because you deserve to grow and you deserve to live your life in a campaign for positive growth in a positive environment.

If you are waiting for an apology, let it go. This apology may come or it may not, but no matter what, forgive them even if they are not sorry.

When you learn to forgive others, even if they are unapologetic for the wrongs that they have committed against you, only then will your mind truly be free. Those who are willing to hold grudges against those who trespass against them are only doing their own selves a disservice. Being unforgiving to someone doesn't benefit any person at all, least of which is you. It causes pain to feel the experience over and over again and that just doesn't need to be thought about on such a high level.

Being unforgiving also tends to distort a person's whole viewpoint. Instead of being able to take risks and see opportunities for what they really are, those who are unforgiving take less risks and only see what life is from their own point of view, since they are less willing to trust in others and their experiences. The negativity that comes from the inability to forgive manifests itself in all areas of life. So forgive, forgive when they apologize, and when they are not sorry and do not apologize, forgive anyway; doing so will free your soul and let you live to reach your greatest potential.

Till today, what my grandmother had taught me has had a very big influence on me and in my practice, working with other people. I often speak in public about being kind, being grateful and being giving. I am often asked: "How do you love if you just have nothing left in you? How could you be strong when your heart is broken and there is no love in you anymore?"

True, how could you love and give when there is nothing left in you? Some people do not want to get hurt, so they would rather hurt others. There are also some people who are afraid of getting hurt and they would rather give up the chance to be happy. Love and hate, they both make people hold on to things, but when love is turned to hate, it becomes a disease that grows inside you until you—and only you—learn to let it go and forgive those that hurt you. Everyone has experienced hurt and suffering in one way or another, the only difference is some people use a magnifying glass to see it, looking at it closely and wondering why every little part affects them, and others see it with a telescope, viewed from afar, as if just one little star in a whole sky full of stars.

I know how that feels. I've been hurt many times. Hurt by actions. Hurt by unkind words. Sometimes, I just don't understand how someone who loves me can do or say such negative things? And it hurts badly, indeed.

But we don't have to take things so personally and painfully. When people insult or mistreat you, don't take offense, don't take it personally, but do listen to their words. They are telling you how they see the world, and they are telling you the exact negative qualities that they possess. In fact, they may not be saying anything about you, but merely negatively reflecting what is in their mind. Maybe they are overweight and don't feel good about it so they say you are fat. Maybe they are upset that they haven't been as successful as they hoped and they take it out on you by saying you are worthless. You know your own value. Don't let their words and actions change what you believe that value to be.

One can only see what's inside them, regardless if it is what is actually present in reality or not. Release the need to feel anger, to want revenge or to hold a grudge. Just say, "This isn't directed to who I am. What goes around comes around." Be kind to them anyway, for they are likely already being punished to live without love and inner peace.

There is a wonderful mythical law of nature that the three things we crave most in life: happiness, freedom, and peace of mind are always attained by giving them to someone else. Some call it karma, a concept of "action" or "deed," understood as that which causes the entire cycle of cause and effect. In simpler terms, it is to do good for others and you in turn will receive good things. Forgive and you will find that doors open. Keep your anger and disappointment bottled up and doors will remain closed. Do good deeds, starting with yourself by allowing you to not be angry, but to be happy. Allow yourself to find freedom in your thoughts and emotions. Allow yourself to have peace of mind; then you will find that life is not only easier, but on a day-to-day basis it is more enjoyable and fulfilling. Then, as you begin giving to others, you will find your life exponentially improved!

This law is an unwritten and pretty much unpopular law with the way that society works today, but it is truly a law that works.

One of the hardest things to do in life is to give away what you have a lack of. If you find yourself lacking in joy or happiness, do your best to make someone else happy. Help someone do something that they would have otherwise never done without your help. Smile and be kind to someone who is being rude to you. Try your best to bless others in any other way that you can think of. You shall find that these actions will come back to you. It may not be tomorrow or next week, but they will return.

If you find yourself lacking peace of mind, help to comfort someone else that you know you can comfort. If you find yourself lacking in freedom, help to give freedom to someone else. Be encouraging and show people the love you have inside of you. Doing these things are good ways to quench your own appetite for happiness, freedom, and peace of mind in your own life.

Many times we don't want to get over all of the pain that we have been through, because doing so requires that we leave behind all of the feelings that require us to face life, so that we can continue to grow.

One thing that we have to remember about life is that if you stop allowing yourself to grow, then you are slowly just dying. When you aren't living a full life there is no middle ground and there is no in-between. It isn't necessary to never remember what you have been through, but it is necessary to take what you have been through, and use those experiences to grow into where you want to go.

It won't always be easy; in fact, it will be quite hard at times. You did your best, to fight, to laugh, to stay positive, to keep hope alive, but to a point you don't know what else you can do. You feel like you had been walking in the dark all alone and you can't see any light ahead. You are scared, you don't want to face your fears, you are afraid of what you may find, and because you are so used to all these negative emotions, you forgot about what it feels like when things were good and bright. I don't have answers for how to make your life better right now, only you have those answers. But I can share with you what I went through. I remember when I came to America, with very little money, broken English, and nobody I knew in this country, the only thing I had in me was being "young, hopeful and fearless," and because I was hopeful and fearless I ended up being in America for 15 years and being who I am today.

Trust me, I am not always tough like many people think. I cry and feel sad, too. The biggest challenge for being a therapist is you wish to find another therapist who can help you when you need someone to talk to. But because you know so much about psychology and the way the mind works, it is even more difficult to find someone you feel is on par or better trained than you are. So I turn inward, seeking answers deep within myself. Here is what I've learned.

The thing that stops us from not going anywhere is holding on to negative thoughts and emotions, especially fear. Fear makes you think about the past, worry about future and blind you to see any open doors in front of you right now. You become stalled, afraid to step forward and even more afraid to step back. But here is the truth: You have to keep moving, even if just one step at time. Nothing is worse than not moving at all. There are going to be people and things that continue to tell you negative things or try to stop you. Be strong and don't let fear overpower you. The feeling of fear and the feeling of excitement to our body's reaction are the same. Next time, when you feel that weird feeling in your stomach again, tell yourself, "I don't fear anything; I am excited because I am ready." Then keep walking. One step after another toward the most positive place you can be. I know it sounds easy ... but what have you got to lose? If you try and fail, at least you've tried. If you try and succeed, congratulations! But if you don't try, you'll never know, will you?

Push fear aside and think positively about what is here for you today and what may come to you tomorrow. Look forward and not backward. Be aware of letting negativity affect you. Stop it in its tracks and take control of your thoughts. Be hopeful and grateful for there is always something to be thankful for in our life. While we often complain about our lives—if only I had a better job, if only I had more money, if only I had a spouse that loved me more--there are people who wish to have lives like us. There are those who barely make it through the week because of lack of food and water and healthcare, and yet here we are, in a prosperous country, with wonderful benefits, and we forget to be appreciative of so much of what we already have. Adjust your attitude and be thankful, and then watch all your pains start to disappear.

I too sometimes have fear of an unknown future, but I like to view it as if I am looking forward to it, not knowing what is ahead and feeling hopeful for it, not afraid. In the meantime, today is all I have, so I try to live it positively as much as I can, remembering that what happened yesterday is in the past and what happens tomorrow is a long way off, but what happens today is what I can live in fully and experience positively if I so choose.

We cannot live life and not get wounded. This is a fact. The point of life is not to figure out how to not get wounded, but to learn to take the moments that wound and quickly heal and continue on; to learn how to assist and encourage others to heal and move forward. As one small drop can make a ripple in the water; one small decision can affect your life in the simplest way. So let's choose to make decisions that are positive and reinforce your goals of happiness, freedom and peace of mind. Things will happen in your life that you can't stop, but that's no reason to shut out the world. There is a purpose for the good and the bad. No matter what way you are going right now, your way is always the right way. You live your life, not someone else. You make your choices, not someone else. You can take bad experiences and learn from them, turning them into good experiences because the next time you're faced with a similar bad situation, you'll know how to deal with it in a more positive manner. Believe in yourself, keep moving forward with love and hope in your heart.

Someday, we'll forget the hurt, the reason we cried, and who caused us pain. We will finally realize that the secret of being free is not holding onto anger or desiring revenge, but letting things unfold in their own way and own time, to be healed and to prove that you can take negative actions and make them work in your favor. In the next few pages you'll learn to start taking negative reactions and turn them into positive actions. You'll start to understand how to turn what you initially thought was a hurtful word and turn it into a positive reinforcement. You'll determine why it is critical to your future happiness to start looking at things in a positive manner and how to turn off anger and make it work in your favor.

Let's get started.

Hatred affects us in a negative way. If you have negative feelings it will not harm anyone else as much as it will harm you. Hence hate is like the parasite that stays inside you and slowly eats away at your core. The person you hate seldom gets affected by your hatred and often does not realize it. It would be appropriate then that hatred toward others should not affect you. Hence you should let go of hate and let love and affection take its place.

Hatred does show negative impacts on our body too. Weight gain due to stress, ulcers, and headaches are the first signs. If hatred is not curbed, it may further lead to depression and high blood pressure. Quitting hatred is like deciding to quit a long addiction of negativity.

Now how do you win over hatred? It is obviously not very easy but many people have conquered the feeling and have become masters of their own selves.

We generally hate people who have left a negative impact on our lives. First of all, we should realize the basic fact that hating people will not benefit us in any way, rather it will only harm us. Moreover, loathing someone just gives the person more power to control us. Often times, they are not even doing anything to force that control, for it is all in our minds. We let our minds dictate our hatred and thus we turn our own thinking against us.

So, are there any emotions and memories you're hanging onto that really should be thrown away? Are there any grudges that need to be forgiven? Are there any negative emotions or resentments that you need to let go of once and for all?

Remember, it's not about what 'someone' did to you, because by hanging onto it ... do you know what you are doing to yourself? If you think I don't understand - that you have a 'right' to hold anger or resentment toward someone, let's consider the story of Steven McDonald:

It was July, 1986. A 29 year old New York police officer by the name of Steven McDonald was walking in Central Park protecting the area from trouble. As he was walking he noticed three young men and thought he recognized them as wanted criminals. So he went to them to ask them a few questions. One of the boys seemed to be hiding something under his clothes. Steven tried to investigate. He was not expecting what happened next. One of the boys pulled out a gun. He shot Steven in the head and neck. Steven fell to the ground, blood pouring from his head.

Doctors worked as hard as they could but could not repair the damage that had shattered his spinal cord. He was paralyzed from the neck down, unable to move for the rest of his life and worse yet, he required a machine just to breathe.

He had been married just eight months to his wife, who was 23 and three months pregnant.

Steven was in the hospital for the next eighteen months. While he was there, his wife gave birth to their baby boy, Connor. The only part of Steven's body with feeling was his face and this is how he felt his son.

At the church for Connor's baptism service Steven talked about the man who had shot him. He said,

"I forgive him. And I hope that he can find peace and purpose in his life."

Steven's statement shocked many people. Many of his friends did not understand why Steven chose to forgive. He explained it by saying,

"I wanted to free myself of all the negative emotions - emotions that this act of violence awoke in me - the anger, the bitterness, the hatred. I needed to be free so that I could love my wife, our child and those around us."

What I love about this is he says that forgiving didn't remove the struggle ... or the questions.

He goes on to say, "We still struggle every day. My wife wants to know why. My son sees other fathers and sons playing. He wants to know why he cannot have those experiences with his father. So we still struggle."

Steven speaks in schools about forgiveness and says, "I often tell people that there is only one thing worse than a bullet in my backbone. That is filling my heart with hate and revenge."

Forgiveness is a subject that people need to hear about today more than ever. As human beings we need forgiveness - we may be giving it - or asking for it. Forgiveness is really about our own healing. We may experience big or small wrongs. But in the end, we choose what we do.

So what can you learn from Steven? Remember, forgiveness is not about the other person - it helps you, and you are doing it for you. The other person doesn't need to even know about it. It can be big things or small, but by forgiving we let go of the past in order to make our future better.

Accept yourself with forgiveness and love. Accept that you are going to make bad judgments from time to time and that the lessons we take from these experiences will help us from making them again. By accepting our own faults we can understand why others have faults of their own and forgive them. To truly forgive the past you must start by forgiving yourself and then you are giving real love, trust, and value. The biggest lesson you can learn is to never lose yourself and that doubting your inner peace will only make you angry, mistrusting, and controlling.

Now, how to be positive if we have learned to let go of negative?

Psychology research estimates that we think between 60,000 - 80,000 thoughts per day and approximately 80% of those thoughts are generally negative. They also say that most of these negative thoughts are the same negative thoughts we had yesterday, last year, and 10 years ago. These negative thoughts have been developing in our subconscious for years, often stemming from childhood issues.

As we age, we tend to repeat the negative thoughts we heard in our childhood and eventually replace our parents' voices with our own. Becoming more aware of your thoughts gives you the freedom needed to alter negative thoughts and replace them with positive ones.

Don't blame yourself for having negative thoughts. We live in an anxiety-provoking world filled with stories of natural disasters, wars and illness. As a result, we are constantly being bombarded with negative and fear-inducing information. It is no wonder we tend to think negatively and are worrying so much of the time.

Life can make you feel lost. It can make you wander around not knowing where you are, what is today and what is tomorrow. Every human being experiences this because it is in our nature: though the lucky ones have the ability to speak their hearts out while others can't and their pain is much more.

Positive thinking has the magic power that you sometimes don't seem to notice. A negative scenario can be dramatically changed with a thought: the same situation with positive attitude can reawaken you and help you overcome any challenge. You wake up in the morning and subconsciously your thoughts determine your action throughout the day. You can't even imagine how little effort you need to achieve what you desire, yet often the first thought when waking up is, "#@&@!* alarm clock!" or "sheesh, another day at work." What if instead you said, "Time to get up. I cannot wait to get started today! I'm going to have a superb day!"

The attitude when you think positively will provide you with the results you want. All you must do is to believe it. Don't be afraid to take to your heart the truth that every time you put positive thinking into your mind, something magical will happen in your life. Your attitude is going to show to the world how important happiness is for you.

If you don't find peace within yourself you will never find it somewhere else. Put that peace inside you by thinking positive thoughts. Push away the negative and accept the positive. You deserve it!

Life cycles will never end. A flower blooms and dies to produce a seed. One seed can start a whole field. There is always a spark of light in the dark, sunrise after a dark night. There is a moon and stars behind that far dark cloud. It's always there even if you can't see it now. Try to find your north star and it will guide you. It's always there in your sky and shines bright. Try to look with an open mind. You need only to realize the truth and believe it's always there. Spread your hands and touch it, grab it and never let it go.

Anything you start to believe in will be reflected in yourself. Humans are complicated; how this thing works, it doesn't matter. Change your thinking and you will find everything in your life changing. It will start by you changing your perception of the things around you, how things will make you realize and find answers. Your worrisome thoughts will start to fade away. Anxiety and deep loop thinking will vanish gradually. You will be able to see things more clearly and begin making positive decisions. You will stop overreacting and bursting out in anger over small things. You will start to feel empathy and put always the positive idea about people around you, which will help you in your life and help you lead a healthier lifestyle.

There are some people whom are bad. It's a fact, and you should learn how to deal with them if it is necessary or ignore and walk away from them if you can. Let your emotional brain have some role in your life and guide you with what is naturally built-in. Some people make you happy, others make you feel bad, get close to the first party and leave the last alone.

Your attitude in life, positive or negative, will impact your health in all areas. Your physical and mental well-being is at stake when it comes to your thinking. When you find yourself thinking negatively, stop yourself abruptly and think of things in your life for which you are thankful. Whether it is having a roof over your head, having food to eat, having good friends to be able to talk to you in your time of need, or the fact that you even have the freedom to pursue your dreams even when your plans aren't going as well as you may have hoped, just be thankful. When the sun goes down, the stars come out. When the stars go away, the sun comes out. Each night and each day you get to start anew.

So smile, laugh, forgive, believe to love and be loved. Always be sure to show compassion and kindnesses to people, for you never know when you may be in the company of an angel ... and by the way, angels don't always have wings, often times they are standing and sitting amongst us, waiting for our asking of them to help.

Our faith can move mountains and the first principle of faith is patience. We give so we get. There is always something in life that makes us smile. No matter how good or bad a situation is, it will change. Love the heart that hurts you, but never hurt the heart that loves you. You know how to do this. You know a different path is possible. Don't hate, just love.

I thank my parents who gave me love and support even when I was the rebellious young girl. I thank them for never giving up on me. I also thank my brothers for their patience and love over the years, even though we have been in different countries for many years.

I also thank my clients, thank you for entrusting me to help you conquer your fears, surpass your expectations, and find your significance. You have taught me much and expanded my commitment to helping more and more people overcome life's challenges. Without you, none of this would be possible.

I have received help, love, support and advice from a few very special individuals who entered my life from nowhere. They have provided unconditional love and strength over many years. I want you to know how much appreciate you. Thank you, a million times thank you.

To my mother and father who through their love and courage gave me the strength to find my life's calling, thank you. To my beloved, dear friends, Jason, Lin, Helen, Amy and Andy who believe in me and challenge me, thank you for your love and friendship. And to all the readers who upon finishing this book will set forth on a new and better life's journey, pursuing and finding your own significance, to love and beloved, thank you for doing your part to make our world a better, more joyful place.

~ Beryl Huang

Deb Wright

DEB WRIGHT, of the Philadelphia Area, is one step closer to living her life full of love by continuing to release the fear-based shackles that have bound her soul in the past. Through the inspirational stories she has shared in her previous two multi-authored books *Step Into Your Best Life* and *Beautiful Seeds of Change*, Deb has been able to cleanse her spirit and embrace personal empowerment by freeing her authentic self from the constraints, judgment and the control of others. With every opportunity she takes, her creative juices and passions flow with ease as Deb enjoys life just being Deb!

justdebb@comcast.net
www.justdebb.net

Unlovable

What Was I Thinking?

Usually my stories start off with a cute little snip-it of a Hollywood chick flick that my readers have probably already seen before. As my written recap paints a mental picture in their heads, I begin describing the correlation between the characters I am talking about in the film and my story I am about to tell. I guess I felt comfortable using this silly little method, because I dream in the exact same way. My dreams are always like I am watching a movie in my mind. I never see my dreams in the first person and I never see things through my own set of eyes either. I watch it all from a distance, like a movie or TV show, I guess it's so I can see clearly everything happening around me. I separate myself in my dreams like a spectator watching a sporting event. As I dream, I can feel my body react with emotion as I watch myself like an actor on a stage. My dreams always feel so real; the situations feel like I am really there. I cry, I sweat, I move and I even scream sometimes as things are playing out right in front of me in my head. This time though, for this story there is no matching movie to start things off. I could not find a perfect fit between a movie and the story I am about to share. Like my real-life experiences on this part of my journey there is no help or visual aid to paint my picture to you. I was and still am on my own to face these things and describe things by myself to the world. It is easy to hide behind a movie avoiding what you don't want to face and it's easy to separate yourself from the direct impact of experiencing something first hand. Hiding IS easy; I have spent my whole life hiding behind "*The Face.*" I know I would rather watch my ugly truth from afar like a movie than face it eye to eye, feel its pain and do something about it to change it. But NOW is the time for me see my own life clearly and for the first time tell my own story in my own words. No more hiding!

When I asked to be a part of this book I apparently was not in my right frame of mind. My story, like everyone else's in this book, is suppose to be an inspiration piece about how we have all chosen to NOT live a fear-based life anymore but instead have chosen to devote our authentic selves to a life filled with love. Who was I kidding; I have no place writing about love! Me and love have to be the biggest joke of the century. I am the last person who should be writing about that!

For those of you who have read my first story, "*The Face,*" in *Beautiful Seeds of Change*, you would totally agree that I have not been someone who has really lived a life of love at all. Instead, I spent most of my life morphing myself into whatever and whoever someone wanted me to be. Relationship after relationship, I would recreate myself to be *their everything* in hopes that they would eventually like me and I would be worthy of their love. Foolishly, I chased the love of others. Dying for a chance at love, I would plaster the perfect face on and make one stupid choice after another, failing miserably at every relationship I attempted. I did everything in my power to feed the desire burning inside of me to be loved. As you can imagine, the void in my soul grew and I became more consumed with filling the emptiness in my heart. I completely believed I needed someone's love in order to feel whole and good about myself. As I got older that craving to be worthy of love turned from a need I was seeking into an ugly form of desperation that I had to fulfill.

With every unsuccessful relationship, I became more desperate. I was convinced there must be something wrong with me. I constantly blamed myself for screwing things up. I analyzed my actions over and over in my head, asking myself, "what if I did *this* better or maybe if I didn't do *that* they wouldn't have left me?" But, the question I asked myself more than any other was, "why didn't they want me anymore?" I wanted to be loved so bad, and the more I wanted it the more my obsession grew. I made the commitment to fixing myself. I made my every thought and action revolve around becoming the perfect people pleaser. I have to tell you, I was good at it... REAL good at it! I never said no, I always put others first, I wanted to be the best at fulfilling everyone's wants and desires, I basically went above and beyond 24/7 no matter what to give them ALL what they wanted. What was I doing? The more I pleased others the more I felt lost, the emptiness continued to grow inside of me until one day I realized I sacrificed everything that I was. Was that really love? I no longer recognized myself in the mirror. I didn't have a mind of my own anymore. I was on autopilot pleasing everyone else all the time but myself. I didn't know anything about myself. Basically I didn't have a clue who I was anymore!

Debbie Doormat

Friends, lovers, co-workers, strangers, honestly it didn't really matter who crossed my path I dumped every ounce of love and energy I had into them. I would lay out of huge buffet of my heart, soul and spirit for them to suck dry until they moved on to someone or something better. I was the master of feeding other's souls, cheering them up, boosting their egos, and making them feel amazing all the while I was empty, starving and completely alone inside. Once I woke up to reality, I realized that it is really hard to tell the difference between someone who loves you for you and someone who only loves you for how you love them. One by one, I looked at everyone in my life and what I found was really sad. Most of the people who I loved really truly didn't love ME at all. They were just energy junkies, sucking the life out of me... taking a hit off the *Debbie Crack Pipe* (as I like to say). I know it's not their fault, how could it be when I was the one filling and filling and filling their cups all up until they were overflowing with love, energy and happiness. They were addicted to my love and positive energy and I was obsessed with giving it to them. Everyone thought I was great and high on life. Always smiling, always laughing and putting on the face that life was so great, I had everyone snowballed. I would always get complimented on how happy I always was and how I would make everyone feel so much better just by being around me. But it was all a lie, I wasn't happy at all deep down inside.

The more I thought I was being loved the more I gave myself to all of them. I just gave and gave and gave to the point of exhaustion. I was drained and empty but somehow I would manage to fill my energizer battery back up and go back out there and do it all over again the next day. I just couldn't help myself. I needed to fill this burning desire to be worthy of someone's love. Looking at the words on these pages and the truth in black and white, I can see how all of you are probably asking yourself, "Why Deb, why do you keep going back for more? You're abusing yourself. They don't love you; they only love the energy you give them!" Trust me I know! You're not the first to tell me this. A dear friend of mine said almost the same exact thing a few months ago. They pointed out (and believe me this was VERY hard to hear); they pointed out that I must think very little of myself to stay in all these unhealthy relationships with people who continually just use me for what I am so easily willing to give them. They even called me pathetic because I clearly have no respect for myself because if I did I wouldn't let people walk all over me like a doormat.

Why do I let people use me like that? Am I really doomed for disaster no matter what kind of relationship I may try to have? I hope the heck not! After writing my first story in *Beautiful Seeds of Change,* I have learned that no one and I mean NO ONE can ever love me if I don't love myself. It took a lot for me to admit that and accept that I was going about love in the completely wrong way. I didn't know how to go about learning how to actually like myself. I was a stranger, a shape-shifter, and most of all a fake in my own life. I was a liar and an actor simulating my way through my journey as the perfect person for everyone else but me. Why was it so easy to make everyone in my life feel like the king of the world and my best friend, but when it came to me I had no idea how to begin to give? I couldn't even look in the mirror. I was disgusted with myself. I didn't want to see the pitiful person looking back at me. Who was Deb? How would I recognize her if I saw her? Hang on I am getting ahead of myself, we will get back to those questions in a few. But that whole mess aside, you really want to know what was even harder for me to cope with more than anything... it was the WHY of it all. Why was it so much more important to me to be worthy of the love of others and not self love?

Why did everyone always come before me? Why was their happiness more important than my own? I lived to please others, love others and devoted my life's purpose to making sure no one ever felt the pain and loneliness I feel everyday in my heart. But I needed to stop that. I needed to stop living through others (you can read more about that part of my journey in my second book *Step into Your Best Life*) and start focusing on MY life! I knew I couldn't just flip a switch and turn off everything I have been for almost 40 years, but I needed to make time for myself. I needed to make time to look at the mess of a life I created, reflect on the bad choices I made, understand why I hurt the people I did along the way and figure out what made me want to repeatedly harm myself over and over again. So I decided to step out of my life for a bit.

I built this huge world made of lies; I was lying to myself, convincing myself I was happy the way my life was and lying to others making them believe I was living a perfect life. I was a fraud dancing my way through life, being everything to everyone no matter who I hurt in the process. And as sad as it is to say, in the moment I didn't feel bad at all. I actually thought I was happy making others feel good and I loved giving them what they wanted. I truly thought it made me happy too. I should have felt guilt and pain for some of the choices I made and I should have felt remorse for the bodies I left in my wake, but at the time I didn't. I didn't care. I didn't feel anything other than that craving for more. I was wrong, I was soooooo wrong! I was way off base, I thought it was what I wanted, and I thought that that's what love was. But once I stopped putting everyone else first and stepped out of my life for a little bit and viewed it like in my dreams, boy did I get a HUGE smack of reality in the face with what I saw.

Red flags went up everywhere! One by one people I once loved and devoted myself to, began to distance themselves from me. Some would get mad at me because I wasn't the, "sure, no problem" girl anymore. People didn't really like me anymore when I stopped being Debbie-Dogooder. They wanted the old me, "anything for you" me and "I am all yours" girl back and not this "no I come first person." Where is the Debbie Doormat we like her better! Where is Here for the Entertainment Deb, get her back! The more people fought against 'me choosing me', the more I saw how people were only in my life to feed off me. Our relationships weren't a two way street, it was a *me give to them* and a *they take from me* relationship. That's not what I want, not anymore. Love doesn't work that way!

As my circle of energy-feeders began to shrink, the more I began to stand up for myself. I started to speak my truth without fear, the more I took back control the more I longed to grow and be free of the shackled life of guilt I once had. So now that I wanted that, I mean REALLY wanted it, I needed to figure out how to go about setting myself free? After continuous months of crying and beating myself up over my failures, I figured out that I really needed professional help. I knew I was a mess and most likely depressed over this realization but I didn't want a doctor doping me all up on meds or forcing me to go back into therapy so, I sat down one day and made a list of five questions. How does a fraud and a liar discover who they really are when they have only lived a fake life of lies? Can I become a good person and learn to be true to myself? How do I become aware that people are using me for the way I love them? How can I learn to love myself? And, am I able to free myself of a life filled with guilt and fear?

meHARMONY

Now that I know that it isn't everyone else's love that I need, how do I find the answers to all the questions I ponder and how do I fill the voids in my life in a healthy way? What I really need to do is love myself unconditionally and BE my authentic self, but how? Obviously it's easier said than done! One morning the universe must have heard my cries because they sent me a sign that was the answer to my prayers. I know there are no such thing as coincidences and everything DOES happen for a reason so I put myself in fate's hands and jumped into this one with both feet. I was sitting in my living room having coffee and looking like a total depressed mess, when on this TV show they were talking about this book that has changed the way people look at themselves and their relationships with others. After listening to success story after success story and the journeys some of these people had been on they managed to find their way to a place of self discovery. I was glued to the TV, they had me hooked. I needed to know more, to know how they did it. I needed this. *This* could be the golden key to release me from my shackles ... I needed this book!!!

I felt a glimpse of life re-enter my 'un-showered-pajamas wearing-depressed mess of a body.' I had motivation to finally leave my safe zone of a house. I decided to get my grungy butt in the shower and head out to the bookstore up the street to get this book. Once I got there I asked the girl where I could find, *Falling in Love for All the Right Reasons by Dr. Neil Clark Warren*. She said to me it was over in the "Self Help." Hmmmm self help... was this another sign? So, I went over to that section of the store where the *eHarmony* book was and began scanning the shelves for it. In my search I stumbled upon this purple spine paperbacked book with a title that captivated me right away, it was called *Dare to Be Yourself by Alan Cohen*. I pulled it out and read the sentence on the front cover, "How to quit being an extra in others people's movies and become the star of your own" and I said to myself, "YEP THAT'S ME!" But more about that book later.

Back to browsing the shelves for the *eHarmony* book. Once I found the book I started thumbing through the pages and read several lines here and there that gave me a totally different outlook on what the book was all about. There was this one line on page 23 in the first chapter that kind of really summed things up for me and reassured me that buying this book was the right thing for what I needed to do in order to begin discovering myself and loving who I was. It said, *"If you don't take the time to know yourself, and you don't know what you want and don't know what kind of person you want to spend your life with, it's not going to work."* I honestly thought this book was going to help me find true love and a soul mate like the cover stated, but instead it was more directed toward teaching you how to know and love yourself FIRST and then be able to share all that you are with that special someone who would love you for YOU! Love starts with me.

I didn't want to make the same mistakes I made in my past relationships and I know it was my own fault of why they failed. As he mentioned in chapter two, I can't have a healthy relationship with anyone if I haven't discovered who I was as a person yet, or what I wanted from life or what values I wanted to live with.

Now I could go on and on about the overall purpose of this monumental book and how it has changed my life for the best, but I am going to let all of you discover its message on your own. I am going to just focus on how it has helped me look at myself as a person and the impact of how it has helped me move toward love. The two particular areas that affected me most and helped heal my soul were the sections on good character and emotional health.

Good Character, I definitely did not have that! I wore "The Face" in all my relationships, transforming myself into their perfect match all the while lying to myself and them about who I was and that I was happy in the relationship. If I could so easily lie like that to other people and act as if *it* was a normal part of my life then how could I call myself a good person? No relationship could ever survive if one of them is a liar. How could anyone ever trust me if I was faking my way through the relationship and justifying my actions with excuse after excuse? Trust is one of the most important things of any relationship. And after reading through this chapter I realized that I was NOT a good person. My desperation to be loved caused me to have a clouded and distorted outlook on what a righteous and genuine relationship should be built upon. My connections with people had no good values, no honesty and no overall basis of good morals and respect. Good character was not something I brought to my relationships nor did I attract from the other person.

As I looked in the mirror I could see that I WAS the main cause of my reoccurring self destruction. I was the kind of person who mastered the art of putting on a façade and faking my way through life. I was so disgusted with myself and truly hated the ugly person I was. It was no wonder everyone left me. I would have left me too. I made myself completely unlovable. I realized that I had way too many character disorders to correct and overcome within myself before I could get involved with anyone, no matter who they were, ever again. I couldn't keep doing this to them or myself anymore. This vicious cycle needed to stop!!! I only have myself to blame and it is up to me to remain this way or not and I definitely don't want to be this bad of a person anymore. I want to be a better person, a good person, I want to speak my truth and have it come from a place of love. I want to love myself, I want to be honest in my relationships and be a person of good character. I have been a monster hiding behind a big glowing smile wearing "The Face" around like an accessory to an outfit. I don't want that anymore. I refuse to live my life based off of lies. I want to love myself, respect myself and project all that I am in a good positive way. I know it is going to take a lot of work and a constant conscious effort everyday to be that better person but I know that I AM ready for the challenge and I AM ready to commit to being the best me possible!

But being a better person was only half my battle. I was emotionally unhealthy ... VERY unhealthy. I believed I needed someone to make me feel whole like in the movie Jerry McGuire "you complete me." Wow was I way off base. I learned in Chapter four, that going into a relationship hoping that some person was going to fill my voids and validate my self-worth was the wrong way to go about satisfying the emptiness yearning in my heart. Putting that kind of pressure on someone to be all the emotional things you are lacking is a recipe for sabotaging anything good about who they are. He talked about how a good relationship has to do with the quality of your self-conception as well as your partners. I didn't even know what self-conception was let alone apply it to a relationship. So, I looked it up and found out that it is the mental image some have of them self based on what their own strengths, weakness, status and overall self-image is. Well, apparently I don't have that! When I see myself, I see an unlovable girl starving for love and attention and who is so desperate to have it that she is willing to give up all that she is for it. Wrong, wrong, wrong, wrong, WRONG!

Good emotional health starts with a good self-concept, and I didn't have one. I couldn't run to a store and just buy one, what I need to do was actually begin to like myself. I needed to like being me and to be comfortable in my own skin. I need to be able to be strong enough to stand alone in life and not be so dependent on others to reinforce my self-worth. He pointed out that people who have a good self-concept possess three important qualities: a sense of significance, truly authentic to themselves, and is a self-giver not a self-seeker.

I don't know if I really have ever had or felt a sense of significance? From my understanding, he suggests that if someone is emotionally healthy they will believe that they will have great intrinsic value. I didn't know what the heck that was so I Googled it. I am really not sure but I think it has something to do with good vs. bad morals and the consequences that come with those actions performed. Basically, what I got out of what I read online is that it goes hand in hand with good moral judgment and the value of it "in its own right." That being said, he goes on about how a person's value is NOT based off of what other people think and say about someone. (This is what I had been doing wrong all along.) And that a person with a solid sense of significance would naturally believe they have been created with great values and they don't need anyone to validate that for them. These people of a solid sense of significance know deep down in their heart that no one can ever take that away from them no matter what. I needed to believe that within myself. I spent so much of my life wanting someone to make me feel worthy that I threw good morals right out the window and didn't give a crap about the consequences that came with my choice. Now I realize that it has been up to me all along to provide it.

I needed to believe in myself, know that I valued myself and I needed to be true to myself. I wanted to begin living my life as the authentic me and devote myself to constantly be true to who I am deep down inside without fear. Authenticity scared me to death considering I spend most of life living one lie after another. After reading this book, and understanding this quality of being my authentic self, I do feel liberated like he said. Living an authentic life really is beneficial; it helped with my healing process and growth. I have made the repeated mistake of being untrue to myself by recreating myself as someone fake and different in all the relationships I have had in my past. Maybe it was a defense mechanism to hide behind or maybe it was a big wall I built around me to protect my fragile heart but either way things needed to change. It has to so I can no longer hide in fear and actually begin to move toward a life of love.

I want to give love freely, not have it taken from me. And in his last quality he talks about just that. He tells me that once I begin to know who I truly am and start living my authentic life, I will be able to give love freely without expecting anything in return and THAT my friends is what I have been doing wrong all along!!! I was doing the opposite, give; give giving and hoping and praying for love in return. No wonder I kept failing in my relationships. Demanding selfish expectations only sets me up for disappointment and that was exactly what I was doing again and again. He goes on to say once I figure this out and learn to give without needing that void filled in return I will naturally attract people who want to give back to me, not take from me. I do want that, oooooo I do, I do! I want to love unconditionally and desire to be someone who can love freely. I want to be emotionally healthy so I can someday find the relationship of my dreams. I know I need to focus on my sense of self-concept and the three qualities it possesses to get to that point. I hope that one day I can share my life and all that I am with someone. And I know it isn't going to be something I can do over night or by the flick of a switch, but I know I can do it. I know it is going to take a lot of time, energy and commitment on my part to get there but I now believe I am worth the effort.

I Double-Dog Dare Ya!

So remember that book I mentioned earlier, *Dare to Be Yourself by Alan Cohen*, well after I started slowly incorporating the eHarmony guy's core values one by one into my everyday life I began reading this book. And one story more than any other touched the deepest part of my soul in the most unexplainable way. Now granted all the stories in this book moved me and inspired me but not like the way this one did. Believe it or not it was the very first story in the book, it was called, "*The Golden Buddha*." It was only three pages long but man did it impact my life. So much so, that I have a Golden Buddha in every room of my house to remind me of this story and the incredible meaning behind it. The story begins talking about this enormous beautiful Buddha made entirely of gold that sits on a hilltop at this monastery somewhere, Thailand I think? It was up there for all to see and for people to come visit anytime they wanted. It truly was a vision of beauty. Sadly, there was word around the village that an army was coming to take over the town so the monks decided to cover the Buddha with mud, rocks and mortar to hide it. This was their way of protecting the Buddha from harm and being destroyed by the invaders. Years passed and the beautiful Buddha remained hidden away from the world, until one day someone saw a glimmer of gold shine through. He called for several other monks to come and help him remove the disguise and help reveal the inner beauty hidden beneath the ugly rock and mud exterior. Before they knew it the rough covering was gone and the beautiful Golden Buddha was back for all the world to see once again.

This story teaches us that behind the walls and facades we build around us to hide and protect who we truly are from the world, lays a bright beautiful soul like the Golden Buddha waiting to be seen and heard. That magnificent spirit who has been hidden away somewhere deep down inside all of us DOES have the strength and power to give and receive love freely. It DOES know the truths of our heart and our authentic selves. This story shows us that we MUST discover and live our truth and go after what our heart desires. We can hide who we are from the world by the protective walls we built around our true selves in fear but we cannot destroy it. Our inner truth is still there, wanting and waiting to be revealed.

Now is my time to let my Golden Buddha shine. I know I need to reclaim my identity, be proud of who I am and all that I have to offer this world. I need to stand tall and proud of my authentic self. I need to shine and dance in the light of my soul's beauty and greatness because I know that I am now worthy of love, the kind of self love that my heart has been aching for all along. I CAN be a good person, and I know some day I can be loved by another because when that day comes I know one day I WILL love who I am too. I don't have to hide who I am anymore, I don't have to be the person I once was or the person I was expected to be. I don't have to live in this mess of a world I created all those years ago. It is my time to remove my shackles and move toward love because I believe that a life without love is no life at all and that life begins with me!

I am so grateful to all the men who my heart has chosen to love along the way; you have all had such an impact on my journey toward life and love in so many ways. From my first crush to where I stand today, it was you Dan who were brave enough to stand by me through the toughest transition of my life and I can't thank you enough for it! And lastly, to my twinflame, whoever you may be, for giving me hope that one day someone will love me as much as I hope to love myself!

My story is dedicated to all the beautiful souls who have had the courage to see past my walls and give my heart a chance at love!

~ Deb Wright

Constance Mollerstuen

CONSTANCE MOLLERSTUEN is a Licensed Heal Your Life® Workshop Facilitator, Holistic Health Coach, author, and the founder of Universal Harmony Holistic Healing Workshops for Life Balance, in Oak Harbor, Washington. She created her company out of her own necessity to live a more balanced happy life. Constance has been inspired to follow her passion which is to assist others on their journey to discover the peace, love, and healing they need in order to live in harmony and attain the joyous, abundant, healthy lives of their dreams.

Connie@holistichealingworkshops.com
www.holistichealingworkshops.com

The Art Of Being Numb– The Bottom Rung

 When I was a child I caught a fleeting glimpse out of the corner of my eye. I turned to look but it was gone I cannot put my finger on it now. The child is grown, the dream is gone. I have become comfortably numb.

~ PINK FLOYD

Of course I had heard of the old saying "Life is what you make it." I guess I just never really realized that someone like me had a choice in the matter. I was too busy letting life happen to me while reacting to all of the circumstances that I thought were out of my control. I was blissfully being the blind observer seeing the outer layer of the experience as it was happening but not really understanding that I could possibly be the orchestrator behind the experience. You can say I was deaf, blind, and comfortably numb. The art of being numb to life had become my normal way of functioning in the world. How else do you make it through the really tough times? I had to show everyone that I was strong and independent and that I could overcome anything that I was faced with, besides no one was there to help me anyway. Everywhere I turned there seemed to be another obstacle to face. I was always told that I did not have the right to FEEL anything; so it was customary for me to shut off my emotions. After all, it was a sign of weakness to be vulnerable. Each time I would experience an emotion it began to feel like a chard of glass sliding down my esophagus slowly cutting me little by little until it plummeted to the bottom of my stomach and gouged out a large chunk. Over time I become so numb that I could no longer feel anything. That was until one day my throat closed off and I was unable to swallow. I could no longer pretend that I did not feel the pain, it was unbearable. All I could think about was how do I make the pain stop and what was the quickest method?

It's hard to actually recall what finally lead up to that point. Looking back there were so many events that had molded me into the person that I had become. As I was running the knife back and forth across my wrist I wondered how hard I had to push. I had never done this before, and I surely didn't want to do it wrong. I just wanted it to be over. I could recall a memory from middle school. A friend of mine accidentally severed her main artery in Art class. We were doing a woodworking project and all of a sudden the chisel slipped and she cut herself. Blood was squirting everywhere. I was sitting next to her and my first reaction was to grab her wrist as tight as I could to stop the flow. I found it a bit ironic that at this time in my life I was searching for that same artery in my own wrist hoping that mine would react the same knowing there was no one there to stop the flow.

"Close your eyes and just do it. What are you waiting for?" I was hunched over in my chair, wrist face up on my lap. As I lifted my head I could see that the walls were still melting. The green, blue and red so bold, so beautiful were mocking me as they slid in and out of the puddle of wall. The longer I stared the more I came to realize they weren't melting after all, they were breathing. In and out, in and out, the rhythm changed and it took me awhile to realize they were mimicking my every breath. I was terrified and quickly looked down. The plush carpet warmed my bare feet and provided a bit of comfort. That was until it started to grow and wrap itself tightly around my ankles. I jumped up in an attempt to loosen their grip. I could see myself in the bathroom mirror, the blade glowing brilliantly in the sun which magnified in the reflection. Who was this person? I could barely recognize her. The new meds were supposed to be a very low dose, something they would gradually increase over time as I needed to control the pain. I was 33 years old and because of a car accident I was doomed to live out the rest of my life in chronic pain. None of the doctors knew what to do with me. They would pass me on from specialty to specialty uncovering yet another symptom which added to the mystery. The test results showed damage to my brain and everywhere they touched me created unbearable misery to the point of almost passing out. I didn't care what they wanted to call it. My blood was boiling fire from hell and fireballs were shooting through my veins and lodging themselves in every organ of my body. It hurt to wear clothes, it hurt to be touched, it hurt to sit, it hurt to stand, it hurt to lie down, it hurt to breathe, and it hurt to be me. The meds were supposed to take the edge off. I had only been on them a few days, weeks, months? I could not recall. My days and nights were melding into one. No matter. Whatever the case may be I was in the bathroom with a knife trying to slit my wrist. In between the confusion the pain and the numbness I heard a faint cry. A tiny sound that shocked me back to reality. It was the baby monitor. My three year old was asleep upstairs, she must have woken up. I washed my face with cold water and told myself to get it together. I hid the knife in the bottom drawer and made my way up to her room. As I arrived I noticed that she was still sound asleep. I was shocked, what did I hear? Am I going crazy? Just then the front door opened. It was my eleven and twelve year old children who were just getting home from school. I started to sob uncontrollably. I did not even realize that if I would have gone through with it my kids would be coming home and walking into that. What kind of mother was I? Without any notice I was enveloped in deep darkness and the pain was gone. I was once again numb. I pulled myself together, drank down a few more chards of glass with that all too familiar flavor and walked down the stairs to greet my children. From that point on I had made the conscious decision to take complete control and turn off my emotions forever. I could never really be certain that it was the meds that brought me to that point or the compounded traumatic events. But, for some reason I was still here. A divine presence worked a miracle for me that day but I was not paying attention.

Reflections On The Art Of Being Numb—One Step Higher

 The thoughts you think are the tools you use to paint the canvas of your life.

~ LOUISE L. HAY

The feelings that brought me to contemplating suicide were real. They may have been chemically induced but I now realize that I have been on the path of self destruction for as long as I can remember. I have to admit I have been sabotaging my health for years. It is really the only thing I felt I had control over. Every time I was upset I would stop eating which eventually lead to the full blown out version of the eating disorder anorexia nervosa. I also used to dream about having a car accident. I hated my job and the people I worked with treated me terribly. My husband was abusing me and I was pregnant with my second child. Eventually my thoughts became my reality and I experienced a life altering car accident. While I was recovering from the accident at home I began to watch the Oprah show. One day her guest was a women named Louise Hay who had written the books *Heal Your Body* and *You Can Heal Your Life*. She was suggesting that your thoughts and feelings behind the thoughts could affect your life either positively or negatively. I had never heard of such a thing. I ordered both of the books immediately and found extreme pleasure in learning this new way of thinking. By doing the exercises in the book I was able to learn what negative beliefs I was carrying with me over the years and learn how to change them so that I could live a more proactive life filled with positive experiences. Each week as I watched Oprah I was introduced to many more amazing authors and soon I had built my arsenal of self help literature. Authors such as Carolyn Myss, Cheryl Richardson, Dr. Wayne Dyer, Gary Zukav, Eckhart Tolle and Deepak Chopra are a few of my favorites. The next step in my healing journey was to learn how to forgive. It was a long process but what I discovered was that the hardest person for me to forgive was myself. When it comes to forgiving someone else I had realized that they may not have even realized they had hurt me. I was holding on to the pain that they caused reliving that memory over and over which kept hurting me more and more. I was punishing myself for something that happened long ago. They didn't even care and had moved on with their lives so why would I want to keep torturing myself? That behavior only builds self-righteous resentment, and that is a terrible way to live. Of course I am not saying that you need to condone someone else's poor behavior; I am saying that you need to let go of the stuff you are holding onto. Everyone, including you, is doing the best they can at any given moment, with the understanding, awareness and knowledge they have. To give up our resentment and replace it with understanding is to free ourselves. Forgiveness is really a gift to ourselves. By using positive affirmations on a daily basis I found it easier and easier to move through the pain and forgive. Here are a few affirmations to start you on your way. "I love and approve of myself and easily make changes," "I live in the present moment and I easily release all past pain and forgive," and "I am willing to experience all the joys of life. Life loves me. I am safe."

Prince Charming—Still On The Bottom Rung

> I always keep running back to the same people because it's safe and it's what I am used to. That's my biggest problem. I will never find my prince until I am strong enough to leave the frog.
>
> ~UNKNOWN

> You tolerate abuse from another just as long as it is a bit less than the degree that you abuse yourself.
>
> ~DON MIGUEL RUIZ

Where O where is my Prince Charming? Somewhere along the line I decided that I needed Prince Charming to rescue me. I thought that one day he would show up on his trusty steed and whisk me away from my terrible life and we would live happily ever after in our beautiful castle in a far away land. I was five years old. He had sandy blonde hair, blue eyes, a great smile and a bit of a tan. I was instantly in love. In order to get his attention, my sister, our friend and I used to take our baby dolls for walks past his house several times a day. One day as we were walking a bee flew by and caught me by surprise. I screamed really loud. This of course got the attention of all of the kids in the neighborhood, including Scott. When they came to investigate, my friend told them that I was scared of a little tiny bee. They all began to laugh and I was humiliated. The next day as we were playing, Scott came up to me slowly and told me not to move. He said there was a bee on my back and if I moved it would sting me. I froze in my tracks.

He would say *don't worry I will try to get it off for you*. This went on for hours it seemed. I would continue to ask if it was gone and he would say no and tell me it was creeping closer to my head or my arm or my ear. I would eventually break down into tears and someone's mother would come to my rescue. This went on all summer and during the next school year. Each time Scott would see me he would tell me that there was a bee somewhere on my body and I would be at his mercy. I did eventually get sick of this game and move when he told me not to and as luck would have it I got stung. So, I never really knew when he was lying and when he was telling the truth.

Could this be my prince? His locker was just around the corner from mine, he had sandy blonde hair, blue eyes, a great smile and a bit of a tan. I was instantly in love. We had no classes together but my friends knew who he was. As time went on we had become very good friends and my love for him grew stronger. Lots of other girls liked him too and they spent a lot of time trying to win him over and rubbing it in my face when they did. Even though we were "just friends" I was devastated but our friendship was strong and I knew that he was always going to be someone important in my life. Because I was afraid that I cared for him more than he cared for me, you know the "just friends" part; I made sure to push him away before I really found out by marrying a man I hardly knew. My first husband was shy and very polite. He thought I was wonderful and I felt sorry for him because he had a bad childhood. He was completely disconnected from his parents and he stuttered when he was nervous. After a year together I found out that I was pregnant so we decided to get married. I loved the idea of having my own family and I could not wait to be a mother. What I did not realize was that my husband had a terrible temper and that he was also a drug addict. After four years of physical and mental abuse and two children later I finally gathered enough nerve to file for divorce. I had finally realized that I could not fix him.

Years passed and I was in the throes of another unhappy abusive marriage. How could this one turn out so bad? He worked hard to take care of us. But, to begin with I was not completely in love with him. I thought that would come with time. After five years of marriage I ended up having a very bad car accident and our life fell apart. He became angrier and angrier and I became sicker and sicker. One day out of the blue I received an email from my friend from high school. He had been thinking about me and wanted to see how my life was going. Of course I did not have many good things to say. I told him I was contemplating divorce but that I was weak and not recovering from my injuries as well as expected. I didn't know how to gain the strength that I needed to begin the process. My friend recommended several books to me that helped him through some tough times in his life and also gave me the name and number of the spiritual counselor he was seeing. After reading the books I started to believe that there could be light at the end of the tunnel. I decided to take the next step and reach out for help, something I never did and called the counselor to make an appointment. Seeking this advice was exactly what I needed. I learned to set boundaries and was able to close that painful chapter of my life. I had a lot of work to do on myself to become whole again. With the help of many wonderful books, my counselor and my dear friend I was finally able to see the good in the world and believe I deserved to live a wonderful happy life.

Once you think you have passed the test you actually get the test. He had blonde hair, blue eyes, a great smile and a bit of a tan. I was instantly in love. He was funny, kind and handsome. He had three children just like me and evidently we went to high school together although he was a few years older. We talked for hours and had a wonderful time. I thought about him a lot but we were both going through divorces and it was not a good time for either of us. We remained friends and talked often. As time went on I discovered that we were not at the same stages in our divorce process. My papers were filed and my court date set. He on the other hand had not even started the paperwork. That of course put a huge damper on the relationship. He was scared to make changes and to move on. He knew he did not love her but he felt obligated to try because he had never put the effort into their relationship like he was with our friendship and he felt extreme guilt. It was the hardest thing I had ever done but I gave him the name and the number of my counselor. They began couples counseling that next week. About once a week my new friend would text or call me to see how I was doing and tell me how things were progressing with his efforts to rekindle something that did not exist. I had started to have real feelings for him and did what I could to support him as I was not ready to let him go. We met for lunch once in a while and before you know it two years had passed. Finally the day I had been waiting for had arrived. He moved out and filed for divorce. He moved in with some friends and then eventually migrated to my house. I was so happy but nervous and uncomfortable at the same time. On several occasions our wonderful evenings would transform into the game of three questions. "Why did you really leave her?" Are you sure you want to be with me?" and "Why did you leave now, are you sure it's really over?" Needless to say this was completely counterproductive and we always ended up in a fight. I guess I pushed his buttons one too many times. Because after about a month of me continually pressing him for the answers to the same questions he left for work one morning and never came back. I was miserable and always thinking the worst. I felt desperate and insecure. I would call and he would not answer so I would leave messages until his phone was so full it would not accept messages any longer. Eventually he would call and tell me he missed me and we would get back together. Finding bliss for a few months but then falling back into the same trap. I would once again feel that strangeness inside and start asking the three questions all over again. He would then leave and a few months later he would come back. We did this dance for several years. That was until one day I finally decided to step up to the next higher rung on the ladder.

Reflections On Prince Charming—One Step Higher

As I move up the ladder I am able to see that my fear of bees was tied into the fear and confusion that I felt when being held captive by the first boy who not only tortured me but was the first boy to kiss me. He was my first love. I believe this is why I learned to accept abusive relationships into my life. He acted as if he cared but would then turn around and treat me badly. Somehow I was able to look past his bad behavior and remember that he really did like me therefore if I doubted his sincerity that would make me the bad guy, right? Low self esteem from being picked on in school and the divorce of my parents lead to the pattern of thinking which formed a deeply ingrained belief. I was not worthy of love. Abuse felt safe because I really didn't have to get too close to anyone especially if they were mean to me. Besides I thought I deserved it because I felt like no one would love me anyway. If by the off chance someone good came into my life I unconsciously sabotaged all chances of happiness by running away or creating conflict. We are spiritual beings having a human experience. It is the destiny of our soul to seek experiences which will help us to grow so that we can realize our true purpose in this life. I was doomed to repeat the negative experiences until I finally learned the lessons I was meant to learn. These lessons bring us closer to our true nature, our divine spirit, LOVE. As humans we tend to focus on the love of outside sources; the love of people, money, material possessions, and job titles. When what we really need is to learn to love ourselves. I kept searching outside for my prince charming when I should have realized he was always right there with me all along. Love needs to be cultivated and nurtured it must be a daily habit so that it becomes a way of life. Once I made the decision to love myself completely and no longer live my life being deaf, blind and numb the universe opened a whole new world of possibilities to me. I finally married the man I pushed away for years. He has been my greatest teacher testing me all of the time yet providing me a safe haven where I can nurture my soul and remember the source from where I come from. Moving toward the love and light that I have within has changed my life forever.

Rethinking an initial reaction to a troubling incident that happened in life is like taking a higher step up a ladder. From that higher perspective, we see farther. We see more. We get a clearer view. A wise way to live is to take this higher step. If something that happens triggers a negative reaction, such as fear or resentment, first we acknowledge the feeling, inviting it to offer its meaning or message to us. Listening, we then move on to have a new, or second, thought about the incident. We pause and renew, centered in the recognition of our divine guidance and truth. A deeper understanding arises when we allow time for the new awareness to well up, as it does gently and easily once we have released any attachment to negative, fear based emotions. When we open to this new, second thought, the wise self is accessed, and we are then equipped to respond to the triggering incident from a higher level of spiritual awareness. We become inspired to choose love and empathy for all concerned, including ourselves. By being willing to wait for this second thought, we move from reactivity, which is always at the same level as the trigger event, to the empowering, higher level of responsiveness. We are guided to do that which leads us even higher in our spiritual evolving.

~ Kathy Juline

Thank you to the many teachers I have encountered on my journey. Overcoming the adversity that I had to face in your presence has helped me to realize what truly matters and what doesn't. Louise Hay, Dr. Patricia Crane, Rick Nichols, and my HYL family your guidance, inspiration, and support have given me the opportunity to fly beyond my wildest dreams. To my family your belief and encouragement has given me the extra self confidence that I needed to step out of my comfort zone to discover and follow my bliss.

Dedicated to everyone who is blindly walking through their lives; May these words of hope and healing guide you toward the insights needed for you to awaken your spirit so that you can let your light shine. Find the courage to release your fear, open your heart and become the LOVE that you seek!

~ Constance Mollerstuen

Elizabeth Candlish

ELIZABETH CANDLISH is the Owner of Sunshine Reiki Healing and is an established Healer, Certified and Licensed Heal Your Life® Teacher, Mentor, Author and Wellness Practitioner in complementary medicine and is based in West Sechelt, on the Sunshine Coast, Vancouver, BC.

Elizabeth is a gifted healer and works with clients using different healing modalities and shares her unique gifts, intuition and inspiration for clients to heal from within.

Elizabeth is a Usui Reiki Master/Teacher and also teaches all levels of Reiki that she also practices herself.

Elizabeth loves travelling with her husband Martin, writing, hiking with friends, and spending time with Cheryl her daughter, and Josh and Fin her grandsons when they come for 6 weeks holiday every year.

eacandlish@dccnet.com
www.elizabethcandlish.com

⚓ Synchronized Moves

Attending workshops was something very new to me - I had only ever attended a Reiki Level One workshop and with only a couple of students attending.

After completing the Reiki workshop I now had a KNOWING feeling that I was going to be doing something else with my life. I had no idea what at that time. Working in a doctor's office was busy and sometimes stressful, so much so that I nearly always worked through my lunchtime - I usually stayed in the office. One day I knew I had to go downstairs and wait in the foyer area. Why? I had no idea but the feeling was so strong that I took my book with me, which just happened to be about Reiki. I was reading and studying for taking my Reiki Level Two, sitting quietly in the foyer area watching as people went in and out of the building. It was as if I was waiting for someone but I had no idea who. Several people passed me by and said "Hi." Some were people I knew and some I didn't and I thought to myself intuitively, "No. It isn't them." The doctor who I worked for had gone over to the hospital in his lunchtime to see his patients and was on his way back to the office. When he saw me he sat down next to me and started chatting, then he got up and went back to his office for a quick lunch. I thought again, "No. It isn't him." Then a friend, who I hadn't seen for a couple of years, stopped by, sat down and we chatted. Then suddenly she noticed the book I was reading and she said, "My sister teaches Reiki and is a

Reiki Master Teacher." She wrote down her name and phone number for me and then left.

I KNEW instantly as soon as she walked away that I could now go back to the office as I felt that Shirley was the person I had been waiting for. Seeing her in our office building was a complete surprise in itself as she didn't live locally, and to be given a new point of contact to continue on this new path I was on.

At that time I had no idea what a difference to my life meeting Shirley on that day would be for me. Now, I know that everything happens for a reason and that there is a time and place for everything - this situation seemed to be synchronized with moving forward.

I contacted Shirley's sister, whose name is Hannelore, and she told me that she no longer taught Reiki but was now teaching a different kind of workshop. Her workshop *Power of Intuition* was a long term workshop over a 6 month period and she recommended that I register for a place as it seemed the perfect fit for me.

I had to think about this as it was very expensive for me at that time, and after a few weeks I decided that meeting Shirley was no coincidence and so I registered for the workshop. I was a bit apprehensive about attending but went with an open mind. At the first weekend meeting I was so happy that I did. I found to my amazement there were 12 people attending. We even had to commit to the 6 month workshop by signing a contract saying that no matter what happened in our lives we would attend on that one special weekend a month.

The initial introduction stage was where we each had the opportunity to introduce ourselves. I noticed one of the ladies really caught my attention when she started to introduce herself as Christine, from the Sunshine Coast. I instantly said out loud "Oh.

My goodness, I would love to live there, it sounds so beautiful." I had no idea where the Sunshine Coast was - I just KNEW it would play a significant role in my life at some point. We had only lived in Canada for 4 years at this time. I never thought it would happen as quickly as it did but that is synchronicity for you.

Over the next 3 months the members of the group were all getting to know each other. Ada, who also just happened to live on the Sunshine Coast, invited the group over to the coast for a 'ladies weekend' in April. I had never been on a 'ladies weekend' before, so this was again something new to me. I think I must have led a very sheltered life up to then; my world was certainly opening up to new opportunities. We then started to make arrangements for that particular weekend. I travelled with a lovely lady named Pearl who was great company, and we had lots to talk about. We reached the Sunshine Coast from Vancouver by ferry. The journey and the ferry ride was so peaceful, I could just feel the energy changing as I got closer to the Sunshine Coast. The scenery was beautiful as we were sailing toward the Sunshine Coast, and I was feeling that the energy was calmer and quieter than Vancouver. I am not sure why I noticed this but I now realize that I am sensitive to energies. We drove off the ferry and as we began our journey on the Sunshine Coast, before we had even driven 1 kilometer, I had a burning desire to put roots down in this special location. "I want to live here," I said suddenly - there is something very special about the Sunshine Coast as I was about to find out.

We all had a great time. Ada invited me and Pearl to stay in her home for the Friday and Saturday evenings. The next morning we were served with homemade fresh scones for breakfast. Ada is a great hostess and such good company. We had a bit of time to do some shopping on the Saturday and I picked up some Realty papers to take back home to show my husband Martin, after all we were moving to the Sunshine

Coast I was so certain of that. We were meant to live on the Sunshine Coast - I loved it so much there that I wanted to take immediate action to extend this peaceful energy into my everyday life.

We were all getting together for the Earth Day dance in the evening and we had a great time dancing the night away. Sunday morning we left early and I was very careful not to forget the Realty papers, after all I was going to live on the Sunshine Coast.

When I arrived home I excitedly told Martin about my trip to the Sunshine Coast and how beautiful it was. Now I have to tell you that our only previous experience with ferries was for the trip duration of almost two hours to Vancouver Island and he couldn't be persuaded to consider the move.

Martin was thinking that it was too far to commute to our jobs in Vancouver and was even less convinced that a commute to and from work was not plausible on a daily basis. I explained to him it was only 40 minutes but he couldn't be persuaded to even to consider the move. Having to travel and rely on the ferry didn't seem a good idea to him at all. A change was coming that would alter his perception; he was to change his mind just a few months later through events that were out of our control.

We had been on a 7 day cruise to Alaska and when we arrived home we found that our home had been broken into, and our cars stolen. We were both devastated about this, as you can imagine. Our home just didn't feel like our home anymore. Someone unknown to us had been in and taken so many things from us including jewelry, CDs, and so much more. We called the police and then contacted insurance companies regarding our lost possessions and our cars. A few days later my car was found and I had to go and see a man named Trevor at the insurance depot. Trevor was quite chatty and told me that the car had not been damaged but that the Radio/CD player and all CD's had been taken.

During this conversation he just happened to mention that he lived on the Sunshine Coast (are you getting goose-bumps?). You can bet I had goose-bumps going up and down my body for the whole of the conversation. He said he lived in Sechelt and travelled every day to his work in Vancouver. My thoughts at that time were "So it *is* possible to commute from Sunshine Coast to Vancouver." It seemed to me that this was another synchronistic event and now was a good time to explore the move I felt so strongly about.

I soon discovered that over 1,000 people commute every day to their place of work in Vancouver. As soon as I arrived home I telephoned our Realtor to ask if she would come to see us and give us an estimate for our home. We arranged a time for her to visit within the next few days. Then I phoned Martin and the first thing he said to me was "Have you been drinking?" I was just so excited. I had a KNOWING feeling that everything was going to work out for our highest good.

Looking back now I see that the Universe certainly had a plan for us to come and live on the Sunshine Coast, and had set the path for us to follow. The Realtor came on the Friday evening and explained everything to us and also she had the papers with her for us to sign. I explained to her that it was only an estimate that I needed at this time as Martin had never been to the Sunshine Coast yet! Martin then said "I will sign the papers" and I will never forget the surprise that I felt and the excitement, it was one step closer to living on the Sunshine Coast. He later confirmed and I was so surprised when he went on to say that he was "going with my intuition."

We decided to go to the Sunshine Coast the following day to have a look around and if Martin didn't like it then the Realtor would shred the papers. We had everything to gain and nothing to lose. As it happened, Martin loved the Sunshine Coast area. We put our home on the market and sold it within 21 days, and found our new home in Sechelt within 10 days. Now if that isn't synchronicity I don't know what is.

When you follow your intuition and inner knowing you never know where it will take you. I am so happy that I followed my intuition and that Martin supported it - what a great and supportive husband he is.

It was a whirlwind time and we moved toward love to the beautiful Sunshine Coast five weeks later.

Since then we have moved three more times on the Sunshine Coast and now live in a beautiful property surrounded by water. We both love it here, and life keeps getting better every day, living in such a wonderful area with great friends. Christine, Ada and I are all still connected, along with so many new friends too. I am so happy that I took the big step of attending the workshop that led me to Christine and Ada and then to the Sunshine Coast.

To Gail and Peter, many thanks to you both, without your kindness in the gift certificate for my birthday for a facial and hot rock massage, my life could have been totally different today. Many thanks to you both for leading me to Reiki in a very special way, which has totally changed my life forever.

To all my clients and students of Reiki, I dedicate this book to you and to my good friend and client June De Graw, without Reiki in my life, I would never have met you and experienced our time together. You were a very special lady in my life and in everyone's life who knew you.

~ Elizabeth Candlish

ꙮ Resources

The following list of resources are for the national headquarters; search in your yellow pages under "Community Services" for your local resource agencies and support groups.

AIDS

CDC National AIDS Hotline
(800) 342-2437

ALCOHOL ABUSE

Al-Anon Family Group Headquarters
1600 Corporate Landing Parkway
Virginia Beach, VA 23454-5617
(888) 4AL-ANON
www.al-anon.alateen.org

Alcoholics Anonymous (AA)
General Service Office
475 Riverside Dr., 11th Floor
New York, NY 10115
(212) 870-3400
www.alcoholics-anonymous.org

Children of Alcoholics Foundation
164 W. 74th Street
New York, NY 10023
(800) 359-COAF
www.coaf.org

Mothers Against Drunk Driving
MADD
P.O. Box 541688
Dallas, TX 75354
(800) GET-MADD
www.madd.org

National Association of Children of Alcoholics (NACoA)
11426 Rockville Pike, #100
Rockville, MD 20852
(888) 554-2627
www.nacoa.net

Women for Sobriety
P.O. Box 618
Quartertown, PA 18951
(215) 536-8026
www.womenforsobriety.org

CHILDREN'S RESOURCES

Child Molestation

ChildHelp USA/Child Abuse Hotline
15757 N. 78th St.
Scottsdale, AZ 85260
(800) 422-4453
www.childhelpusa.org

Prevent Child Abuse America
200 South Michigan Avenue, 17th Floor
Chicago, IL 60604
(312) 663-3520
www.preventchildabuse.org

Crisis Intervention

Girls and Boys Town National Hotline
(800) 448-3000
www.boystown.org

Children's Advocacy Center of East Central Illinois
*(If your heart feels directed to make a donation to this center,
please include Lisa Hardwick's name in the memo)*
616 6th Street
Charleston, IL 61920
(217) 345-8250
http://caceci.org

Children of the Night
14530 Sylvan St.
Van Nuys, CA 91411
(800) 551-1300
www.childrenofthenight.org

National Children's Advocacy Center
210 Pratt Avenue
Huntsville, AL 35801
(256) 533-KIDS (5437)
www.nationalcac.org

Co-Dependency

Co-Dependents Anonymous
P.O. Box 33577
Phoenix, AZ 85067
(602) 277-7991
www.codependents.org

Suicide, Death, Grief

AARP Grief and Loss Programs
(800) 424-3410
www.aarp.org/griefandloss

Grief Recovery Institute
P.O. Box 6061-382
Sherman Oaks, CA 91413
(818) 907-9600
www.grief-recovery.com

Suicide Awareness Voices of Education
Minneapolis, MN 55424
(952) 946-7998

Suicide National Hotline
(800) 784-2433

DOMESTIC VIOLENCE

National Coalition Against Domestic Violence
P.O. Box 18749
Denver, CO 80218
(303) 831-9251
www.ncadv.org

National Domestic Violence Hotline
P.O. Box 161810
Austin, TX 78716
(800) 799-SAFE
www.ndvh.org

DRUG ABUSE

Cocaine Anonymous National Referral Line
(800) 347-8998

National Helpline of Phoenix House
(800) COCAINE
www.drughelp.org

National Institute of Drug Abuse
(NIDA)
6001 Executive Blvd., Room 5213,
Bethesda, MD 20892-9561, Parklawn
Building
Info: (301) 443-6245
Help: (800) 662-4357
www.nida.nih.gov

EATING DISORDERS

Overeaters Anonymous
National Office
P.O. Box 44020
Rio Rancho, NM 87174-4020
(505) 891-2664
www.overeatersanonymous.org

GAMBLING

Gamblers Anonymous
International Service Office
P.O. Box 17173
Los Angeles, CA 90017
(213) 386-8789
www.gamblersanonymous.org

HEALTH ISSUES

American Chronic Pain Association
P.O. Box 850
Rocklin, CA 95677
(916) 632-0922
www.theacpa.org

American Holistic Health Association
P.O. Box 17400
Anaheim, CA 92817
(714) 779-6152
www.ahha.org

The Chopra Center at La Costa Resort and Spa Deepak Chopra, M.D.
2013 Costa Del Mar
Carlsbad, CA 92009
(760) 494-1600
www.chopra.com

The Mind-Body Medical Institute
110 Francis St., Ste. 1A
Boston, MA 02215
(617) 632-9530 Ext. 1
www.mbmi.org

National Health Information Center
P.O. Box 1133
Washington, DC 20013-1133
(800) 336-4797
www.health.gov/NHIC

Preventive Medicine Research Institute
Dean Ornish, M.D.
900 Brideway, Ste 2
Sausalito, CA 94965
(415) 332-2525
www.pmri.org

MENTAL HEALTH

American Psychiatric Association of America
1400 K St. NW
Washington, DC 20005
(888) 357-7924
www.psych.org

Anxiety Disorders Association of America
11900 Parklawn Dr., Ste. 100
Rockville, MD 20852
(310) 231-9350
www.adaa.org

The Help Center of the American Psychological Association
(800) 964-2000
www.helping.apa.org

National Center for Post Traumatic Stress Disorder
(802) 296-5132
www.ncptsd.org

National Alliance for the Mentally Ill
2107 Wilson Blvd., Ste. 300
Arlington, VA 22201
(800) 950-6264
www.nami.org

National Depressive and Manic-Depressive Association
730 N. Franklin St., Ste. 501
Chicago, IL 60610
(800) 826-3632
www.ndmda.org

National Institute of Mental Health
6001 Executive Blvd.
Room 81884, MSC 9663
Bethesda, MD 20892
(301) 443-4513
www.nimh.nih.gov

SEX ISSUES

Rape, Abuse and Incest
National Network
(800) 656-4673
www.rainn.org

National Council on Sexual Addiction
and Compulsivity
P.O. Box 725544
Atlanta, GA 31139
(770) 541-9912
www.ncsac.org

SMOKING

Nicotine Anonymous World Services
419 Main St., PMB #370
Huntington Beach, CA 92648
(415) 750-0328
www.nicotine-anonymous.org

STRESS ISSUES

The Biofeedback & Psychophysiology Clinic
The Menninger Clinic
P.O. Box 829
Topeka, KS 66601-0829
(800) 351-9058
www.menninger.edu

New York Open Center
83 Spring St.
New York, NY 10012
(212) 219-2527
www.opencenter.org

The Stress Reduction Clinic Center for Mindfulness
University of Massachusetts
Medical Center
55 Lake Ave., North
Worcester, MA 01655
(508) 856-2656

TEEN

Al-Anon/Alateen
1600 Corporate Landing Parkway
Virginia Beach, VA 23454-5617
(888) 425-2666
www.al-anon.alateen.org

Planned Parenthood
810 Seventh Ave.
New York, NY 10019
(800) 230-PLAN
www.plannedparenthood.org

Hotlines for Teenagers
Girls and Boys Town National Hotline
(800) 448-3000

ChildHelp National Child Abuse Hotline
(800) 422-4453

Just for Kids Hotline
(888) 594-KIDS

National Child Abuse Hotline
(800) 792-5200

National Runaway Hotline
(800) 621-4000

National Youth Crisis Hotline
(800)-HIT-HOME

Suicide Prevention Hotline
(800) 827-7571

A Call For Authors

Most people have a story that needs to be shared—could **YOU** be one of the contributing authors we are seeking to feature in one of our upcoming books?

Whether you envision yourself participating in an inspiring book with other authors, or whether you have a dream of writing your very own book, we may be the answer **YOU** have been searching for!

Are you interested in experiencing how sharing your message will assist with building your business network, which in turn will result in being able to assist even more people? Or perhaps you are interested in leaving a legacy for your family and friends? Or it may be you simply have an important message your heart is telling you to share with the world. Each person has their own unique reason for desiring to become an author.

Our commitment is to make this planet we call "home" a better place. One of the ways we fulfill this commitment is assisting others in sharing their inspiring messages.

We look forward to hearing from you.

Please visit us at

www.visionaryinsightpress.com

CPSIA information can be obtained at www.ICGtesting.com
Printed in the USA
BVOW11s0515210414

351160BV00005B/22/P